COUNTRIES
OF THE
WORLD

D1586185

KINGFISHER

First published 2017 by Kingfisher
an imprint of Macmillan Children's Books
20 New Wharf Road, London N1 9RR
Associated companies throughout the world
www.panmacmillan.com

978-0-7534-4228-9

Consultant: Kimberly Weir
Text written by Mary Budzik
Maps © Cosmographics Ltd.

Dedicated to Kas & Leigh, Ella & Jos, Anais, Manon & Lou

9 8 7 6 5 4 3 2 1
1TR/1016/HH/UG/128MA

A CIP catalogue record for this book is available from the British Library.

Printed in China

Contents

Introduction

Step into Basher's world and meet the characterful countries of the United Nations (UN), all jostling for space across the globe's continents. The UN is an international organization with roots in World War II. A "country", meanwhile, is any region that is run by its own government. The idea is that countries belonging to the UN try to avoid warfare and do all they can to make sure their people have equal rights and opportunities. That's what the countries have in common with each other. This book, on the other hand, considers the things that make them distinct. So let's find out what they're all about.

Arctic Ocean

Chukchi Sea

Beaufort Sea

Baffin Bay

Greenland (Denmark)

Alaska (U.S.A.)

Bering Sea

Gulf of Alaska

Hudson Bay

Labrador Sea

Canada

United States of America

Atlantic Ocean

Tropic of Cancer

Hawaii (U.S.A.)

Gulf of Mexico

The Bahamas

Mexico

Cuba

Dominican Republic

Haiti

St. Kitts & Nevis

Antigua & Barbuda

Puerto Rico

Dominica

St. Lucia

Belize

Jamaica

Guatemala

Honduras

Caribbean Sea

Grenada

Barbados

St. Vincent & The Grenadines

El Salvador

Nicaragua

Trinidad & Tobago

Costa Rica

Panama

Venezuela

Guyana

Suriname

Colombia

French Guiana

Equator

Galápagos Islands (Ecuador)

Ecuador

Kiribati

Pacific Ocean

Peru

Brazil

American Samoa

Bolivia

Cook Islands (New Zealand)

French Polynesia

Paraguay

Tropic of Capricorn

Pitcairn Is. (United Kingdom)

Chile

Argentina

Uruguay

Falkland Islands (United Kingdom)

Arctic Ocean

Greenland
Sea

Barents
Sea

Kara
Sea

Laptev
Sea

East Siberian
Sea

Bering
Sea

Arctic Circle

Sweden   Finland

Russia

North
Sea

Sea
of
Okhotsk

Iceland

United
Kingdom

Rep. of
Ireland

Denmark

Netherlands

Baltic
Sea

Estonia

Germany   Poland

Belarus

Ukraine

Russia

Kazakhstan

Mongolia

North
Korea

Sea
of
Japan

Liechtenstein

Switzerland

Andorra

France

Belgium

Austria

Hungary   Romania

Moldova

Georgia

Armenia   Azerbaijan

Uzbekistan

Kyrgyzstan

South
Korea

Japan

Portugal   Spain

Monaco

San
Marino

Vatican
City

Italy   Croatia   Serbia

Bosnia   Montenegro

Albania   Bulgaria   Greece

Turkey

Black Sea

Caspian
Sea

Turkmenistan

Tajikistan

China

East
China
Sea

Pacific

Ocean

Morocco

Tunisia

Malta

Cyprus

Mediterranean Sea

Syria

Lebanon

Israel

Iraq   Iran

Afghanistan

Pakistan

Nepal   Bhutan

Taiwan

Canary
Islands

Algeria   Libya   Egypt

Jordan

Kuwait

Bahrain   Qatar

Saudi
Arabia

Red
Sea

U.A.E.

Persian Gulf

Oman

Gulf of Oman

India

Bangladesh

Myanmar

Philippine
Sea

Cape
Verde

Mauritania   Mali   Niger   Chad   Sudan

Eritrea

Yemen

Arabian
Sea

Bay of
Bengal

Thailand

Vietnam

South
China
Sea

Philippines

Marshall
Islands

The
Gambia

Senegal

Burkina
Faso

Gulf of Aden

Djibouti

Cambodia

Guinea-
Bissau

Guinea

Sierra
Leone

Liberia

Ivory
Coast

Ghana

Nigeria

Central
African Rep.

South
Sudan

Ethiopia

Somalia

Sri
Lanka

Maldives

Malaysia

Brunei

Singapore

Palau

Micronesia

Gulf of
Guinea

Equatorial
Guinea

Cameroon

Uganda

Kenya

Nauru

Kiribati

São Tomé &
Príncipe

Gabon

Dem. Rep.
of the
Congo

Rwanda

Burundi

Tanzania

Java Sea

Indonesia

Banda
Sea

Papua
New Guinea

Solomon
Islands

Tuvalu

Seychelles

Comoros

East
Timor

Arafura Sea

Coral
Sea

Angola

Zambia

Mozambique Channel

Madagascar

Indian Ocean

Mauritius

Vanuatu

Fiji

Tonga

Namibia   Zimbabwe

Botswana

Australia

Swaziland

South
Africa

Lesotho

Great
Australian Bight

Tasman
Sea

New
Zealand

Southern Ocean

⭐ Look for this symbol throughout the book.
It shows the capital city of each country.

North America

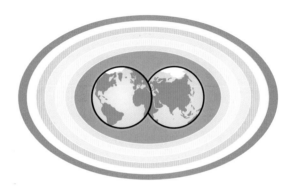

I'm no kid. Some of my rocks are the oldest in the world – four billion years old to be exact! And I can be extreme at times . . . after all, you'll find 149,340 square kilometres of land ice in Canada, while Death Valley in the United States holds the record for the highest temperature recorded on the Earth (57 degrees Celsius, in 1913). But my 23 countries are one big melting pot!

People have come from all over the world to make my homelands their home, bringing their own cultural flavours. It doesn't hurt that much of my topography is roomy and well watered. Complex river systems and huge lakes help keep the land fertile for agriculture and support the wonderful creatures that inhabit my lush forests – from the subarctic north to the tropical south.

* **Land mass:**
  24,709,000 sq km
* **Number of countries:** 23

* **Biggest lake:** Superior
* **Longest river:** Mississippi
* **Highest mountain:** Denali

North America

Antigua & Barbuda

Bahamas, The

Barbados

Belize

Canada

Costa Rica

Cuba

Dominica

Dominican Republic

El Salvador

Grenada

Guatemala

Haiti

Honduras

Jamaica

Mexico

Nicaragua

Panama

St. Kitts & Nevis

St. Lucia

St. Vincent &
The Grenadines

Trinidad & Tobago

United States of America

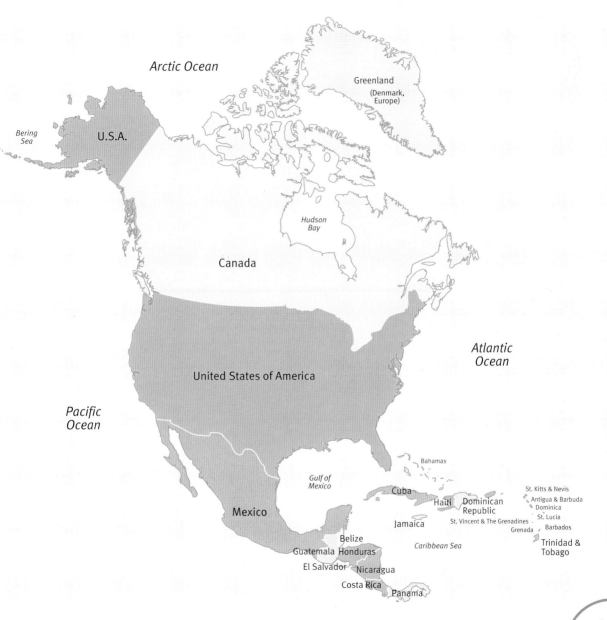

Arctic Ocean

Greenland
(Denmark,
Europe)

Bering
Sea

U.S.A.

Hudson
Bay

Canada

Atlantic
Ocean

Pacific
Ocean

United States of America

Gulf of
Mexico

Bahamas

St. Kitts & Nevis

Antigua & Barbuda

Dominica

Cuba

Haiti

Dominican
Republic

St. Lucia

Mexico

Jamaica

St. Vincent & The Grenadines

Barbados

Belize

Grenada

Trinidad &
Tobago

Caribbean Sea

Guatemala Honduras

El Salvador   Nicaragua

Costa Rica

Panama

United States of America

NORTH AMERICA

* The capital, Washington, D.C., is home to the president's residence – the White House
* New York's Statue of Liberty is one of the country's best-known sights
* The cable cars in San Francisco are the only historic landmarks in the U.S. that move

I'm so large and diverse, everybody dreams of getting to know me, but how? Start up high, I say! Scale my heights for city views – from Chicago's Willis Tower to San Francisco's Transamerica Pyramid. Or clamber up mountains mighty (the Rockies) and old (the ancient, eroded, coal-pitted Appalachians).

Take a grand tour, beginning down south in the Florida Everglades, my largest tropical wilderness, or visit the Mississippi Delta, once the haunt of bluesmen. Channel the writer Mark Twain by taking a riverboat down the Mississippi River. Canter on a paint horse across the desert to the Four Corners – the arid, rugged point on the Colorado Plateau where New Mexico, Colorado, Arizona and Utah meet. But show respect – this is Navajo territory: after the Cherokee of my south-east, the Navajo are my second-largest native tribe. Step onto the glass floor of the Grand Canyon Skywalk, 610 metres above ground, or try your luck with a roll of the dice at Las Vegas. Heading north to my buffalo-roaming plains, stop in South Dakota to see my monumental rock sculptures: first, legendary Sioux chief Crazy Horse, and farther east, four presidents carved into the side of Mount Rushmore. Peckish? Finish up in corn-growing Iowa, home to the country's oldest popcorn factory.

○ **SIZE:**
9,833,517 sq km

◐ **POPULATION:**
323,996,000

○ **CURRENCY:**
U.S. dollar

● **CAPITAL:**
Washington, D.C.

○ **LANGUAGE:**
English

Charters of Freedom

Three documents have shaped the laws of this country and influenced the rights of its citizens: The Declaration of Independence, the Constitution and the Bill of Rights (the first ten amendments to the Constitution).

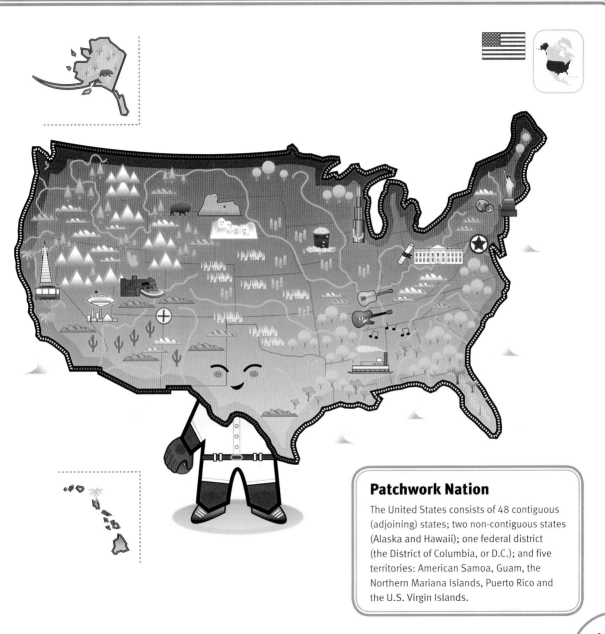

Patchwork Nation

The United States consists of 48 contiguous (adjoining) states; two non-contiguous states (Alaska and Hawaii); one federal district (the District of Columbia, or D.C.); and five territories: American Samoa, Guam, the Northern Mariana Islands, Puerto Rico and the U.S. Virgin Islands.

Canada

NORTH AMERICA

* British Columbia's Kootenay National Park includes both glaciers and cacti
* A town in Alberta built a municipal landing pad for extraterrestrial spaceships
* Poutine – French fries and cheese curds covered in gravy – is a popular Canadian dish

Chilled! That's me. A no-drama kind of country – unless my ice hockey teams aren't doing well, of course. I'm the world's second-largest country in area, but my entire population is less than L.A. and New York combined. Eighty per cent of my people live within 100 kilometres of the U.S. border – the world's longest international frontier! Just check out my territory – it covers four biomes, or ecosystems. From my north, the Arctic chilly, treeless tundra gives way to dense conifer forest. South of here, where it is slightly warmer, more deciduous trees grow and the forest runs into rolling prairies. You can imagine the wildlife – from polar bears to deer, hawks and wolves. Out west, the Rocky Mountains cut through British Columbia; lying to my south the Great Lakes (Superior, Michigan, Huron, Erie and Ontario) form the world's largest group of freshwater lakes.

For centuries, my indigenous people travelled in canoes and on dog-powered sleds. These days, folk are more likely to take the 8030-kilometre Trans-Canada Highway to get from A to B. Crossing all ten provinces from Pacific to Atlantic, it connects all my major cities. In Quebec, don't be fooled into thinking you're in France; it was a French colony for more than 200 years, and French is still widely spoken.

○ **SIZE:**
9,984,670 sq km

◐ **POPULATION:**
35,363,000

○ **CURRENCY:**
Canadian dollar

● **CAPITAL:**
Ottawa

○ **LANGUAGES:**
English, French

First Nations

The indigenous population of Canada includes the Inuit, Native Indians and Métis (those with European and Indian ancestry). Today, these groups account for around one million people.

Tar Sands

Bitumen: sounds like spitting, but is so much more valuable. My midwestern province, Alberta, has the world's largest deposit of this heavy, semi-solid petroleum – unrefined oil. It is formed from the decayed organic matter of an ancient sea that covered the area around the time of the dinosaurs.

Mexico

NORTH AMERICA

- ✴ The ancient Olmecs carved massive stone heads – some as tall as 3 metres
- ✴ Parícutin, one of the world's youngest volcanoes, emerged as recently as the 1940s
- ✴ Corn originated in Mexico more than 7000 years ago

Imagine this: life without chocolate, corn or chilli peppers. That's right, I introduced those delights to the world. I've been here for millennia – long before the Spanish explorer Hernán Cortéz arrived in 1519.

From skinny north-western Baja California to the Yucatán peninsula in my south-east, I manage to squidge no fewer than nine geographic regions between my Atlantic and Gulf of Mexico coasts – that's no mean feat. Expect to see the Rio Grande and Colorado Rivers, arid coastal plains, scorching deserts, lush mesas (flat-topped hills) and volcanic mountains. More? Sure. How about touristy Acapulco beaches, a Copper Canyon and a limestone karst riddled with sink holes. Oh, and I have resources a-plenty: silver, lead, zinc, copper, tin and oil.

My people go back a long, long way. The Olmec civilization from my south lays claim to being the earliest in the Americas (around 1200 B.C.E.). Succeeding the Olmecs, were the Mayans, Aztecs and Toltecs, among other awesome civilizations. Mexico City, my great contemporary capital, was established on the ruins of Tenochtitlán, the ancient Aztec capital that was thriving in 1519 . . . until Hernán Cortéz burned it down.

SIZE:
1,964,375 sq km

POPULATION:
123,167,000

CURRENCY:
Mexican peso

CAPITAL:
Mexico City

LANGUAGE:
Spanish

Play Ball!

The Olmecs invented the rubber ball and used it to play *tlachtli*, a game that was a little like basketball (get the ball through a ring) and a little like football (no hands). Losers were sacrificed to the gods!

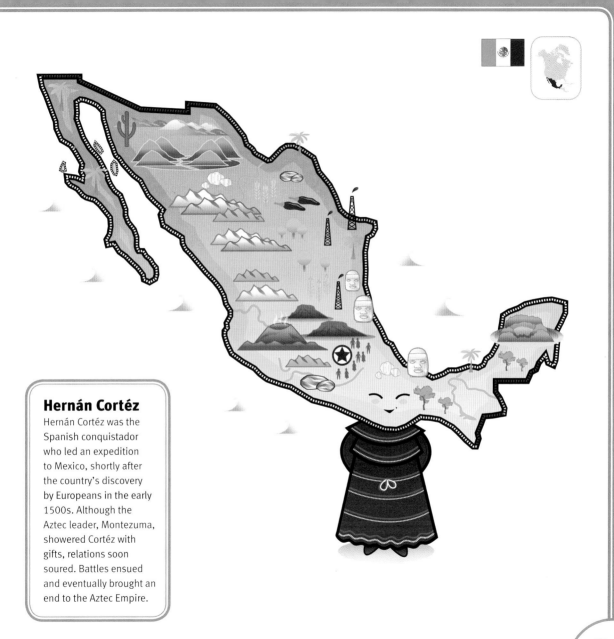

Hernán Cortéz

Hernán Cortéz was the Spanish conquistador who led an expedition to Mexico, shortly after the country's discovery by Europeans in the early 1500s. Although the Aztec leader, Montezuma, showered Cortéz with gifts, relations soon soured. Battles ensued and eventually brought an end to the Aztec Empire.

Belize

NORTH AMERICA

* Sugar, bananas and citrus fruits are among Belize's main exports
* Part of the Belize Barrier Reef, the Great Blue Hole is the largest sink hole in the world

My species tickle your tongue and strike sparks in your eyes . . . trees include allspice, calabash, frangipani and soursop. I count the tapir, margay and gibnut among my animals. And my national flower is the black orchid – sounds like it could slay you, no?

I sit on the east coast of Central America. My northern territory is all limestone lowlands and swamps. Toward the south, I rise up to the rugged Maya Mountains, with Victoria Peak their highest point. Dense jungle fills my interior and the Belize Barrier Reef, the world's second-longest, lies just off my shores. Mayans inhabited me from 1500 B.C.E. – their legacy is the ancient site of Caracol in my Cayo District. Millennia later, European settlers known as Baymen established logging colonies to harvest my logwood tree. Its extracts are used for dye and to indicate acid levels for medical tests. In 1840, I was colonized by British people searching for mahogany wood in my dense forests – they left the English language as their legacy.

SIZE:
22,966 sq km

POPULATION:
354,000

CURRENCY:
Belizean dollar

CAPITAL:
Belmopan

LANGUAGES:
English, Spanish, Creole

Guatemala

NORTH AMERICA

I'm popping with volcanic mountains, earthquakes and Caribbean coastal hurricanes! In the jungle lies the ancient Mayan city of Tikal. One kind of forest wasn't enough for me: I've got mangrove, cloud, rain and pine. Even my animals specialize – in names with intense spelling: try *phyllomedusa*, quetzal and jaguarundi. I stay chilled by chomping gum: one of my exports is *chicle*, sapodilla tree sap used to make chewing gum.

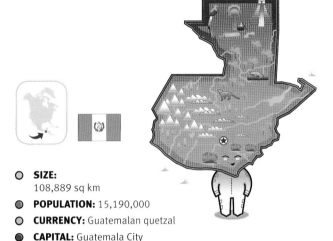

- **SIZE:** 108,889 sq km
- **POPULATION:** 15,190,000
- **CURRENCY:** Guatemalan quetzal
- **CAPITAL:** Guatemala City
- **LANGUAGES:** Spanish, Amerindian

El Salvador

NORTH AMERICA

Notched into the Isthmus of Panama, I'm the smallest, most densely populated Central American country. If I am not suffering storms at the hands of El Niño, I'm quaking in seismic fear of volcanic activity. My ancient city of Joya de Cerén bears witness to this and is likened to Italy's Pompeii. Other features include my coffee plantations and the beloved sea turtles – four of the world's eight species – who've made me their home.

- **SIZE:** 21,041 sq km
- **POPULATION:** 6,157,000
- **CURRENCY:** U.S. dollar
- **CAPITAL:** San Salvador
- **LANGUAGE:** Spanish

Honduras

NORTH AMERICA

- The mountains in Honduras make up 80 per cent of the country's terrain
- Mahogany used for Gibson guitars is sustainably logged in the Honduran rainforest

SIZE:
112,090 sq km

POPULATION:
8,893,000

CURRENCY:
Honduran lempira

CAPITAL:
Tegucigalpa

LANGUAGE:
Spanish

Christopher Columbus himself named me. In 1502, on his final voyage, he landed on my Caribbean coast and noticed the waters were unusually deep. *Honduras* means "depths" in Spanish, hence my name.

I'm almost completely surrounded by water, with the Caribbean Sea to the north and the Pacific Ocean to the south. More than half of my border with Nicaragua consists of water – the Coco River. Inland from Mosquito Coast, once home to the Mosquito Indians, my Río Plátano Biosphere Reserve is a whopping 5250 kilometres of rainforest, roamed by the mantled howler monkey, the giant anteater and the brown-throated sloth. Elsewhere, my forests of pine and oak have been logged for growing bananas and coffee – major exports of mine. Close to my border with Guatemala lies the ancient Mayan city, Copán.

Nicaragua
NORTH AMERICA

* Nicaragua's northern tamandua looks like an anteater wearing a panda-bear coat
* Agricultural crops include corn, beans, plantains and cassava

I am Central America's largest country and my north-eastern coastline gets the most rainfall in the whole region. Having said that, in times of drought – as a water-saving tip – my people are advised to keep and eat iguanas instead of chickens. Yum!

Take it from the pirates who loved me – I'm a tropical hotspot – literally. My earth bubbles with volcanic energy. To my west, nineteen active volcanoes form a belching, boiling chain from north-west to south-east. That's not all bad; I'm working on harnessing their energy to give my people access to geothermal power, and the weathering of volcanic ash makes my soils rich and fertile. Besides volcanoes, I'm known for my lakes. Lago de Nicaragua, my enormous interior lake, boasts as many as 365 islets, two volcanic islands (Ometepe and Zapatera) and even the occasional bull shark! In the olden days, the lake was connected to the Pacific by a stagecoach line run by Cornelius Vanderbilt, an American tycoon!

○ **SIZE:**
130,370 sq km

◑ **POPULATION:**
5,967,000

○ **CURRENCY:**
Nicaraguan córdoba

● **CAPITAL:**
Managua

○ **LANGUAGE:**
Spanish

Costa Rica

NORTH AMERICA

Check out my numbers! I occupy 0.03 per cent of the Earth's surface, but contain six per cent of its biodiversity. And I am committed to preserving that environment; hydroelectric plants generate four-fifths of my electricity. I enjoy a tropical climate and six of my fourteen volcanoes are active. Not fiery enough for you? Check your sandals before putting them on – when my bullet ants bite, the pain rivals that of a gunshot.

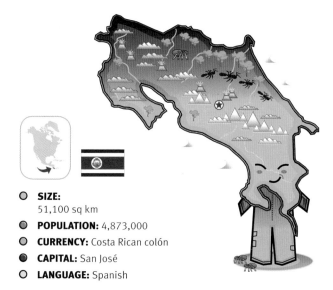

- **SIZE:** 51,100 sq km
- **POPULATION:** 4,873,000
- **CURRENCY:** Costa Rican colón
- **CAPITAL:** San José
- **LANGUAGE:** Spanish

Panama

NORTH AMERICA

See my skinny waist, the Isthmus of Panama? Its canal (built in 1914) makes for a great short cut between the Atlantic and Pacific Oceans. Mountains form my spine, while dense tropical forest makes up 40 per cent of my land. Hundreds of unique species thrive there, including my national flower, a white orchid called Flor del Espíritu Santo (Flower of the Holy Spirit). Oh, and with more than 500 rivers, I'm no stranger to hydroelectric power.

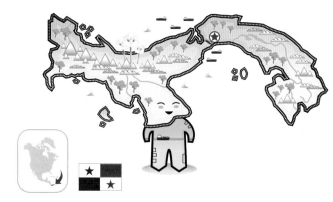

- **SIZE:** 75,420 sq km
- **POPULATION:** 3,705,000
- **CURRENCY:** Panamanian balboa, U.S. dollar
- **CAPITAL:** Panama City
- **LANGUAGE:** Spanish

Cuba

* Cuba is home to classic dance styles that include the mambo and cha-cha-chá
* Baseball is the favourite sport of Cuban people

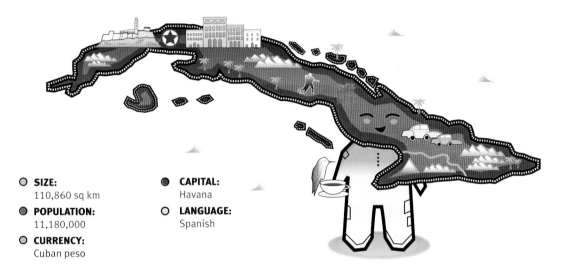

○ **SIZE:**
110,860 sq km

◉ **POPULATION:**
11,180,000

○ **CURRENCY:**
Cuban peso

● **CAPITAL:**
Havana

○ **LANGUAGE:**
Spanish

Separated from Key West, Florida, by a 160-kilometre strait, I'm the largest island in an archipelago that is also called Cuba. My mountainous coastlines give way to a mostly flat terrain, dotted with limestone hills.

Before Columbus arrived in 1492, the indigenous Taino and Ciboney tribes occupied my land. Spanish colonizers set up sugar and coffee plantations, and my port of Havana was where ships departed for Spain, laden with New World riches. Today, Havana harbour is guarded by a turreted fortress built to scare away pirates. Since my Communist revolution of 1958, modernization has been minimal, and today I feature classic old buildings painted in Easter egg colours and lovingly maintained 1950s American cars. My 300 native bird species include the world's smallest – the bee hummingbird.

Dominican Republic

NORTH AMERICA

I make up half of Hispaniola Island – the better half, obviously, since I'm the most visited island in this sea. Even Christopher Columbus stopped by, in 1492. Do people come to see the Caribbean's tallest mountain (Pico Duarte) and its largest lake (Enriquillo)? Or perhaps they are attracted by my year-round golf courses? I like to think the lure is my lively music, *merengue típico*, which features the *güira* – a perforated metal scraper played with a brush.

- ○ **SIZE:** 48,670 sq km
- ◐ **POPULATION:** 10,607,000
- ○ **CURRENCY:** Dominican peso
- ● **CAPITAL:** Santo Domingo
- ○ **LANGUAGE:** Spanish

Haiti

NORTH AMERICA

The smaller half of Hispaniola, I was once a French colony and the New World's richest. In 1801, I became the first New World country to abolish slavery. Since then, hurricanes have blown and earthquakes rumbled across my mountainous terrain, yet my people walk tall (balancing water jugs on their heads). My brightly painted homes show my cheerful spirit, while the practice of voodoo gave rise to the legend of zombies.

- ○ **SIZE:** 27,750 sq km
- ◐ **POPULATION:** 10,486,000
- ○ **CURRENCY:** Haitian gourde
- ● **CAPITAL:** Port-au-Prince
- ○ **LANGUAGES:** French, Haitian Creole

Jamaica
NORTH AMERICA

- ❊ At the Hope Botanical Gardens you can see the blue mahoe, Jamaica's national tree
- ❊ Jamaica's giant swallowtail is the western hemisphere's largest swallowtail butterfly

○ **SIZE:**
10,991 sq km

◉ **POPULATION:**
2,970,000

○ **CURRENCY:**
Jamaican dollar

● **CAPITAL:**
Kingston

○ **LANGUAGES:** English,
Jamaican Patois

Lying 145 kilometres south of Cuba, I'm an island crossed from east to west by the forested Blue Mountains that are famous for their high-quality coffee.

I've got a lilt all my own, a beat as jaunty as my percussive reggae and a flavour that's as sweet, hot and bubbly as my ginger beer. You see, African slaves created my culture. Imported by my Spanish and English colonizers to work on sugar, cocoa and coffee plantations, through agitation and escape they made me their own and created a culture with African roots and Caribbean flavour. Today, I've got a vibrant music culture and an eye-opening cuisine: mannish water, a stew, is made with all parts of the goat (including feet). The ackee, my national fruit, is only for the initiated: eat the wrong parts, and you might get Jamaican Vomiting Sickness.

The Bahamas

NORTH AMERICA

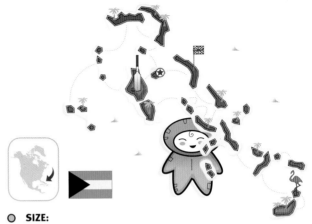

A British colony since 1783, I didn't gain my independence until 1973 – the Brits are gone, but cricket is here to stay. An Atlantic archipelagic state, I consist of 700 islands, cays (low islands), and islets. *Bahamas* means "shallow water" in Spanish; the differences in depth of sea around my cays (reflected in its colours) can be seen in photos from space. Be sure to go to the island of Great Inagua – home to some 50,000 flamingos, my national bird.

- **SIZE:** 13,880 sq km
- **POPULATION:** 327,000
- **CURRENCY:** Bahamian dollar
- **CAPITAL:** Nassau
- **LANGUAGE:** English

Antigua & Barbuda

NORTH AMERICA

A dorable twin islands, we've been an independent state within the British Commonwealth since 1981. Known for our intricate coastlines, we are said to have 365 beaches – one for each day of the year. Sadly, the good life we offer is threatened by sea-level rise and drought – the two of us are short of rivers, lakes and streams. A number of our species are at risk too, including the yellow-breasted Barbuda warbler.

- **SIZE:** 442.6 sq km
- **POPULATION:** 94,000
- **CURRENCY:** East Caribbean dollar
- **CAPITAL:** St. John's
- **LANGUAGES:** English, Antiguan Creole

Barbados
NORTH AMERICA

※ You can take a tour of 2.4-kilometre-long Harrison's Cave by tram

※ The blind, burrowing Barbados threadsnake is about the size of a 10-pence coin

I'm sweet! That's me alright, oozing sugar and molasses since the British arrived in 1627. I'm situated in the western North Atlantic, north-east of Venezuela; my British colonial history is evident in the cricket greens and Episcopalian churches that dot my villages. My name means "bearded ones" – figure that out! The name likely refers to the aerial roots of my native bearded fig tree, which resemble bundles of grizzled, grey hair hanging beneath the foliage.

Mostly flat, I'm composed of coral-reef limestone (or sediments deposited over centuries by decayed sea-creature skeletons) and am riddled with caves – 85 of them, in fact. Animal Flower Cave, my only sea cave, features sea anemones that disappear into stalks when threatened. Compared to nearby islands, I have few endemic, or native, species – that's partly due to people introducing non-natives that take over, and partly because I am younger than my neighbours. My only truly native mammals are bats!

○ **SIZE:**
430 sq km

◑ **POPULATION:**
291,000

○ **CURRENCY:**
Barbadian dollar

● **CAPITAL:**
Bridgetown

○ **LANGUAGES:**
English, Bajan

Dominica

NORTH AMERICA

☀ Columbus named the island for the day on which he discovered it – Sunday (in Italian)

☀ Dominica's biggest exports are bananas and soap

A mountainous isle of rainforests, natural hot springs, sulphur vents and a boiling lake, I've got a full head of steam. Located between the Caribbean and the North Atlantic along with Guadeloupe and Martinique, I became the last Antilles island to be settled by Europeans, because my native Kalinago (Carib) people put up a good fight. The Kalinago called me Waitukubuli – "tall is her body" – because of my steeply ridged, forested terrain. Despite colonization, my Carib people live on – the only remaining pre-Columbian population in the entire Caribbean. Way to go, guys!

Be warned! You'll not catch a tourist bus to my Boiling Lake in the Morne Trois Pitons National Park; instead, embark on a mucky hike through the fumarole-ridden Valley of Desolation. My carnival showcases original folk music developed by descendants of the West African slaves. Expect such sounds as jing ping, bouyon and a dance known as the flirtation.

○ **SIZE:**
73,757 sq km

◉ **POPULATION:**
74,000

○ **CURRENCY:**
East Caribbean dollar

● **CAPITAL:**
Roseau

○ **LANGUAGES:**
English, Dominican Creole

Grenada

NORTH AMERICA

I'm a diddy little island chain whose capital nestles neatly in a natural harbour. Pretty, pastel-coloured houses rise up the hillsides from the sea. I'm known as "spice island": pantries far and wide are stocked with the nutmeg, allspice and ginger that flourish here due to my climate, rainfall and volcanic ash-enriched soil. Chocolate, too. Oil Down, my national dish, is a stew of breadfruit and meat seasoned with the yellow spice turmeric.

- ○ **SIZE:** 344 sq km
- ◉ **POPULATION:** 111,000
- ○ **CURRENCY:** East Caribbean dollar
- ● **CAPITAL:** St. George's
- ○ **LANGUAGES:** English, Grenadian Creole

St. Kitts & Nevis

NORTH AMERICA

Two volcanic islands in one sovereign state, we are separated by 3 kilometres of water. We happen to major in coconuts. Small and round, Nevis amounts pretty much to the sum of its only mountain, Nevis Peak. The more shapely St. Kitts has a ridge of volcanoes down its back; the highest – Mount Liamuiga – has a lake in its crater. The two of us sit in a tropical hurricane zone. Things get wet and windy between August and October.

- ○ **SIZE:** 168 sq km and 93 sq km
- ◉ **POPULATION:** 52,000
- ○ **CURRENCY:** East Caribbean dollar
- ● **CAPITAL:** Basseterre
- ○ **LANGUAGE:** English

St. Lucia

NORTH AMERICA

I have subterranean minerals, gases and mud that refuse to stay put. That's right, I'm home to Sulphur Springs, otherwise known as the "drive-in" volcano: you can walk right through the crater. Heat from deep in the Earth's core bubbles up through my steam vents. Luckily, the blue-headed, red-breasted, green-backed jacquot – my native parrot – prefers to perch in my interior rainforest, a safe distance from any boiling potholes.

○ **SIZE:**
616 sq km
◉ **POPULATION:** 164,000
○ **CURRENCY:** East Caribbean dollar
● **CAPITAL:** Castries
○ **LANGUAGES:** English, French Patois

St. Vincent & The Grenadines

NORTH AMERICA

B lessed or cursed? You decide. My Carib natives called me Hairouna, "Land of the Blessed". My volcanic soil is so rich, it's said a pencil would sprout and grow in it, but a volcano's blessings are mixed: In 1902, an eruption killed 1680 people. King's Hill Reserve in Kingstown is the western hemisphere's oldest botanic garden; it was established after a drought, on the assumption that preserving trees would increase rainfall.

○ **SIZE:**
389 sq km
◉ **POPULATION:** 102,000
○ **CURRENCY:** East Caribbean dollar
● **CAPITAL:** Kingstown
○ **LANGUAGES:** English, Vincentian Creole

Trinidad & Tobago

✳ Endangered leatherback sea turtles use Trinidad's Matura Beach as a nesting site

✳ Calypso music and steel-drum bands originated in Trinidad & Tobago

We're siblings, so we love to tease. Just ask us! Trinidadians will say that Tobagans are too serious. Tobagans will say that Trinidadians need to stop shaking to a calypso beat and get in line. But we love each other, really – you can call us Trinbago!

Trinidad lies just 11 kilometres off the Venezuelan coast – its Northern Range of mountains is simply a continuation of the Andes. Down south, thanks to gas and water seepage (euch!) the island is known for its mud volcanoes. Tiny Tobago carries the Andes even farther, its Main Ridge sloping down to sugarcane-growing plains. We love red around here! You can't miss the clear reddish-orange of Trini's national bird, the scarlet ibis, or the evil red sting of the scorpion – the Trinidad Moruga pepper that is officially the world's hottest. Cool your tongue with our purple-red sorrel drink, distilled from roselle, a kind of hibiscus flower. Have a glass and *lime* with us – that's Trinbago speak for "hanging out".

○ **SIZE:**
5128 sq km

◉ **POPULATION:**
1,220,000

○ **CURRENCY:** Trinidad and Tobago dollar

◉ **CAPITAL:**
Port of Spain

○ **LANGUAGE:** English

South America

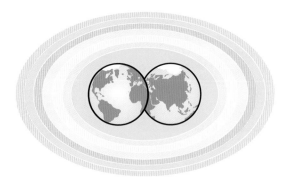

Does any other continent match my geographical wealth? From my belly full to the brim with the fat Amazon rainforest to my tiny, island-studded tip named for flames – Tierra del Fuego – I am a continent bursting with tremendous vitality. Even the textiles produced by my indigenous people are fabulously colourful! You may say I'm boastful, but the fate of the world could depend on me.

Think about it: one-fifth of the world's oxygen is produced in my rainforest. Charles Darwin, father of the science of evolution, formed his theory of the natural selection of species after visiting my Galápagos Islands. Even my deserts are chart-topping: outside of Antarctica, Chile's Atacama Desert, in the rain shadow of my Andes Mountains, is the driest non-polar place on the Earth.

* **Land mass:** 17,840,000 sq km
* **Number of countries:** 12

* **Biggest lake:** Maracaibo
* **Longest river:** Amazon
* **Highest mountain:** Aconcagua

South America

Argentina

Bolivia

Brazil

Chile

Colombia

Ecuador

Guyana

Paraguay

Peru

Suriname

Uruguay

Venezuela

Caribbean Sea

Venezuela

Guyana

Suriname

French
Guiana

Colombia

Ecuador

Peru

Brazil

Bolivia

Paraguay

Chile

Pacific
Ocean

Uruguay

Argentina

Atlantic
Ocean

Venezuela

SOUTH AMERICA

- Anacondas, the world's largest snakes, live in the Orinoco River basin
- General Rafael Urdaneta Bridge, named for a war hero, is 8.7 kilometres long

SIZE:
912,050 sq km

POPULATION:
30,912,000

CURRENCY:
Venezuelan bolivar

CAPITAL:
Caracas

LANGUAGE:
Spanish

I know all about steep drops, thanks to Angel Falls, the world's highest uninterrupted waterfall. Another drop – in the price of oil – hasn't worked out for me, though. That viscous liquid should be my fortune. My Orinoco Belt contains the largest proven oil reserves in the western hemisphere, but low prices combined with my government's mismanagement have left many of my people facing poverty.

Thankfully, my natural strengths don't fail me. In my north-west, Lake Maracaibo is South America's largest lake. In my centre, more than 2000 tributaries riddle my Orinoco River basin. Running across my interior, the Guiana Highlands underpin the largest undamaged tropical rainforest in the world. And then there is Mount Roraima. This *tepui*, or tabletop mountain, marks a triple border point for me, Guyana and Brazil.

Guyana

SOUTH AMERICA

I was once a colony of the Netherlands, which explains the name of my city, New Amsterdam, famous for its mission chapel. But who needs the city life, when most of my land is forested? Stroll on a treetop walkway in my Iwokrama rainforest; safe from the jaguars below, you might spot a toucan. Rivers flow here, too. My Demerara River gave its name to the colony that founded my thriving sugarcane industry – mmm, those sweet crunchy crystals.

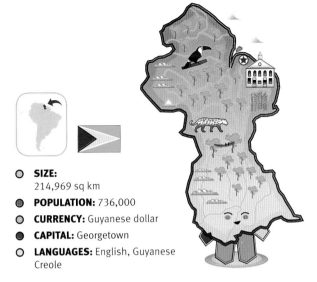

- ○ **SIZE:** 214,969 sq km
- ◑ **POPULATION:** 736,000
- ○ **CURRENCY:** Guyanese dollar
- ● **CAPITAL:** Georgetown
- ○ **LANGUAGES:** English, Guyanese Creole

Suriname

SOUTH AMERICA

I'm the only Dutch-speaking country in South America (once I was a colony of the Netherlands). I'm small, but fiery! Every *Oud Jaar* (Old Year, but actually New Year), ribbons and ribbons of red firecrackers snap, crackle and sizzle in my capital. My two mountain ranges give way to rainforest and savannah; Tafelberg, a heavily forested, waterfall-rich mesa, is probably full of undiscovered plant and animal species.

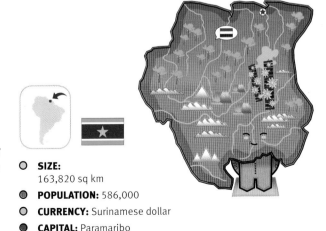

- ○ **SIZE:** 163,820 sq km
- ◑ **POPULATION:** 586,000
- ○ **CURRENCY:** Surinamese dollar
- ● **CAPITAL:** Paramaribo
- ○ **LANGUAGE:** Dutch

Colombia

SOUTH AMERICA

* Ciudad Perdida ("Lost City") dates from 800 c.e. and contains 200 structures
* Andean spectacled bears inhabit Puracé National Natural Park

I'm in chains! Three parallel longitudinal chains of the Andes Mountains, called *cordilleras*, stretch across me diagonally north to south. Known as the Occidental (Western), Central and Oriental (Eastern) cordilleras, they feature peaks as high as 5700 metres. Bogotá, my capital, perches on a plateau in the Oriental cordillera; at 2800 metres, it's the third-highest capital in the world.

East of the mountains, rainforests and plains dominate my territory, covering about three-fifths of my total area. But jungles aren't the only green around here: I am the world's largest source of emeralds, especially the prized Trapiche gemstones found only in mines on the western side of the Eastern cordillera. And finally, wait for it . . . I'm bicoastal! There's the Caribbean to my north and the Pacific Ocean out west. It's on my Caribbean coast that you'll find the walled city and fortress of Cartagena – the continent's most strongly fortified city.

○ **SIZE:**
1,138,910 sq km

◑ **POPULATION:**
47,221,000

◐ **CURRENCY:**
Colombian peso

● **CAPITAL:**
Bogotá

○ **LANGUAGE:**
Spanish

* The once-lost Inca city of Machu Picchu sits up high in the Andes Mountains
* Cerro Blanco in Nazca is the highest sand dune in the world

With more than 90 different microclimates, I'm hard to pin down weather-wise, but I can promise you this: visit me, and 4000 varieties of potato, yellow underpants and roasted guinea pig (including feet!) will be yours to enjoy.

The details: I'm situated in western South America, with a coastal plain bordering the Pacific, the Andes Mountains inland and the Amazon Basin to the east of the Andes. The Norte Chico civilization on my arid, north-central coast is the oldest known civilization in the Americas – thriving around 3500 B.C.E. (the same time the Egyptians were building the Pyramids). About the guinea pig: called "*cuy*", it's a traditional Andean dish, as are potatoes of every colour and stripe. Andean Indians became the first to domesticate the potato by selective breeding: the wild plant is toxic. Without them, the world would be French-fry-less. Yellow underpants? Any self-respecting Peruvian street stall sells them at New Year; they're considered good luck.

○ **SIZE:**
1,285,216 sq km

◉ **POPULATION:**
30,741,000

○ **CURRENCY:**
Peruvian sol

◉ **CAPITAL:**
Lima

○ **LANGUAGES:**
Spanish, Quechua, Aymara

Ecuador

SOUTH AMERICA

Let's set a few things straight. First, Mount Everest may have the highest elevation, but my Mount Chimborazo is the world's tallest when measured from the Earth's core. And Panama hats? Sure, first sold in Panama, but made by Ecuadorean artisans! Country with the world's greatest biodiversity per square kilometre? Yeah, me. World's largest exporter of bananas? Me. Only country named for the Equator (which actually runs through me)? All me, me, me!

- **SIZE:** 283,561 sq km
- **POPULATION:** 16,081,000
- **CURRENCY:** U.S. dollar
- **CAPITAL:** Quito
- **LANGUAGE:** Spanish

Chile

SOUTH AMERICA

Long, slender and slinky, I'm the narrowest country in the world, lining South America's Pacific coast from Peru to Cape Horn. What can I tell you? My Atacama Desert is the driest place on the Earth. My earthquakes often hit 9.5 on the Richter scale. And Gran Abuelo, a native Fitzroya tree of mine, is 3622 years old. Meanwhile, on my remote Easter Island in the south-eastern Pacific, big-headed statues represent the godlike ancestors of the Rapa Nui people.

- **SIZE:** 756,102 sq km
- **POPULATION:** 17,650,000
- **CURRENCY:** Chilean peso
- **CAPITAL:** Santiago
- **LANGUAGE:** Spanish

Bolivia

SOUTH AMERICA

* La Paz has the world's highest seat of government (3650 metres above sea level)
* People dressed in zebra suits work as road-crossing guards

Deep underground, in shafts and tunnels, that's where you'll find my story. Colonial rulers exploited my veins of silver and tin – and my indigenous peoples – for centuries. Cerro Rico, Potosí's rich mountain, was known as the mountain that eats men, but now it's eating itself. It's been so heavily mined that its peak is caving in. Still, my people have ways to resist: they turn to El Tio, a devilish god who guards the mines.

Above ground, my Salar de Uyuni, the world's largest salt flat, is so reflective it's used to calibrate satellites from space. Take care not to stray into its forest of giant cacti! These spiky types grow slowly – just 1 centimetre a year – but reach heights of 312 metres. Ouch! My Altiplano is the world's most extensive high plain outside Tibet. The pink flamingos here are real, not lawn ornaments, and chinchillas are rodents, not coats. And Bolivian women always express their independent style with a gracious tip of their bowler hats!

○ **SIZE:**
1,098,581 sq km

◉ **POPULATION:**
10,970,000

○ **CURRENCY:**
Bolivian boliviano

◉ **CAPITAL:**
La Paz (administrative),
Sucre (constitutional)

○ **LANGUAGES:**
36 official languages,
including Spanish,
Quechua and Aymara

Brazil
SOUTH AMERICA

* Taking up half the continent of South America, Brazil is more than 50 per cent rainforest
* Brazil's football team has qualified for every World Cup to date and has won five times
* Rio de Janeiro's Statue of Christ the Redeemer is one of Brazil's best-known landmarks

Let's face it. Big and resource rich, I am a match for any of the big world players – and not just in the football stadium. The fifth-largest country in the world by area *and* population, I cover four time zones and border all other countries in South America . . . well, apart from Ecuador and Chile!

I've got beaches, rainforests and most of the Amazon River. The Pantanal at my centre is the world's largest tropical wetland. You'll see jaguars, toucans, caimans and many other species here. But I'm not all wilderness and jungle. My two biggest cities, Rio de Janeiro and São Paulo, are humongous, too.

Did I mention my resources? Once the Portuguese "discovered" me in around 1500 C.E., it was game on. Initially, the Europeans exploited my Pau Brasil tree (yes, I'm named for a tree!), but that tree signified just the beginning. In the 17th century, explorers discovered emeralds and gold in my Minas Gerais region. After that, over 13,600 kilograms of gold a year was exported to Europe. Two of my most important exports, coffee and rubber, dominated the 19th century – especially after Charles Goodyear found a way to make my natural rubber durable enough to make automobile tyres, in 1844.

- ○ **SIZE:**
  8,515,770 sq km
- ◉ **POPULATION:**
  205,824,000
- ○ **CURRENCY:**
  Brazilian real
- ◉ **CAPITAL:**
  Brasília
- ○ **LANGUAGE:**
  Portuguese

Carnival
Every year, street parties take over Brazil's cities at the start of Lent. The most famous happens in Rio de Janeiro, where people dress up and dance in the streets to the steady beat of drums.

Woody Emblem

The Pau Brasil is the country's national tree. *Pau* means "wood" in Portuguese and *Brasil* comes from the Portuguese word for "ember"; the reddish wood of the tree, resembling embers, yielded a valuable red dye and the wood is prized for the bows used to play stringed instruments.

Paraguay

SOUTH AMERICA

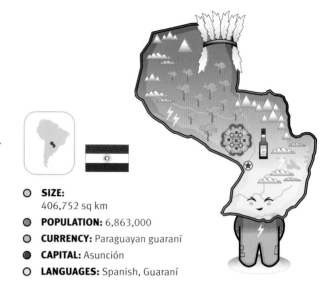

From north to south, I'm sliced right down my centre by the Paraguay River, my lifeblood. I use its mighty force to create hydroelectric power (and lots of it). I'm also a producer of "green gold" (soy) – the world's fourth-largest producer, in fact. To relax, I get caught up in the vivid colours of *ñandutí* (spiderweb) lace-making, or craft vibrant feather capes and headdresses like the ones worn by my native shamans.

○ **SIZE:**
406,752 sq km
◉ **POPULATION:** 6,863,000
○ **CURRENCY:** Paraguayan guaraní
● **CAPITAL:** Asunción
○ **LANGUAGES:** Spanish, Guaraní

Uruguay

SOUTH AMERICA

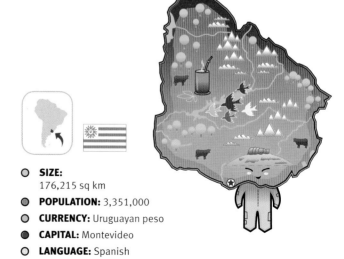

Located on the south Atlantic between Argentina and Brazil, my high point is the curious Cerro Catedral (Cathedral Hill). Otherwise, I'm rocking, rolling pampas (plains) where cows outnumber people. My name means "river of painted birds" for the migrating flocks that fly over my long coastal lowlands. We like herbs here: Yerba maté tea sipped through a bombilla (straw), from a gourd (hollowed-out fruit) thermos, is my national drink.

○ **SIZE:**
176,215 sq km
◉ **POPULATION:** 3,351,000
○ **CURRENCY:** Uruguayan peso
● **CAPITAL:** Montevideo
○ **LANGUAGE:** Spanish

Argentina

SOUTH AMERICA

☀ Elephant seals, fur seals, penguins and sea lions swim off the coast of Patagonia

☀ Gauchos, like American cowboys, symbolize the open plains of the Pampas region

Sink or soar – you choose! The options? Well, you can rise up to Aconcagua, in my western Andes; this "sentinel of stone" is the highest mountain in the western hemisphere. Or you can sink down to Laguna del Carbón, a salt lake in cold, arid Patagonia that also happens to be the lowest point in the western hemisphere. I like extremes, you see; just take my tango, a ballroom dance that originated in the Buenos Aires slums.

Hired assassins! That's what my polo players are called when they play overseas. They perfected their game on my south-western pampas, home to more hard riders: my *gauchos* (cowboys). Seeking more thrills? Why not speedboat under Iguazú Falls – with 275 cataracts, they are twice as tall and three times wider than Niagara! Or head to the Valdes Peninsula in Patagonia for a spot of whale-watching. And you can always dip your toes into the Atlantic at Tierra del Fuego. This "fiery land" is the archipelago at the southernmost point of the Americas.

○ **SIZE:**
2,780,400 sq km

◑ **POPULATION:**
43,887,000

○ **CURRENCY:**
Argentine peso

● **CAPITAL:**
Buenos Aires

○ **LANGUAGE:**
Spanish

43

Europe

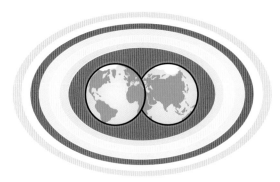

Pack 'em in! I rank third in continental population and contain 45 countries. My people are famous as sailors – to satisfy their wanderlust, they had to take to ships. Starting with the Vikings, their seafaring prowess is legendary! At home, my people consoled themselves with castles – turreted towers teetering on crags and magnificent moated manor houses in ancient fairytale forests.

Try mapping my coastlines: with peninsulas and fjords, islands and inlets, channels, firths and forths, there's not a straight line to be seen! I've also known some colossal collisions in my time: my Alpine mountains are an ancient continental pile-up, the rocky wreckage left behind when the European and African tectonic plates crashed into each other millions of years ago.

- ☀ **Land mass:** 10,180,000 sq km
- ☀ **Number of countries:** 45

- ☀ **Biggest lake:** Ladoga
- ☀ **Longest river:** Volga
- ☀ **Highest mountain:** Mont Blanc

Europe

Albania

Andorra

Austria

Belarus

Belgium

Bosnia & Herzegovina

Bulgaria

Croatia

Cyprus

Czech Republic

Denmark

Estonia

Finland

France

Germany

Greece

Hungary

Iceland

Arctic Ocean

Kara Sea

Barents Sea

Iceland

Norwegian Sea

Sweden

Finland

Norway

Atlantic Ocean

Estonia

North Sea

Latvia

Denmark

Lithuania

United Kingdom

Russia

Rep. of Ireland

The Nether-Lands

Belarus

Germany

Poland

Belgium

Luxembourg

Czech Republic

Ukraine

Liechtenstein

Slovakia

Bay of Biscay

Austria

Hungary

Moldova

Switzerland

Slovenia

Romania

France

San Marino

Croatia

Bosnia & Herzegovina

Serbia

Caspian Sea

Andorra

Monaco

Italy

Monte-Negro

Bulgaria

Black Sea

Portugal

Spain

Vatican City

Albania

Macedonia

Greece

Mediterranean Sea

Malta

Cyprus

Ireland, Republic of

Italy

Latvia

Liechtenstein

Lithuania

Luxembourg

Macedonia

Malta

Moldova

Monaco

Montenegro

Netherlands

Norway

Laptev Sea

Poland

Portugal

Romania

Russia

Russia

Bering Sea

San Marino

Sea of Okhotsk

Pacific Ocean

Serbia

Slovakia

Slovenia

Spain

Sweden

Switzerland

Ukraine

United Kingdom

Vatican City

Iceland
EUROPE

- Icelanders must choose a baby's name from a government-approved list
- Eight per cent of Icelanders believe in mythical *huldufólk* ("hidden people", or elves)

○ **SIZE:**
103,000 sq km

◉ **POPULATION:**
336,000

○ **CURRENCY:**
Icelandic króna

◉ **CAPITAL:**
Reykjavík

○ **LANGUAGE:**
Icelandic

My name says it all! When I was first inhabited, foxes were the only other land mammals roaming my icy terrain. Over the millennia, humans also introduced farm animals, reindeer and mink.

I sit smack on top of the Mid-Atlantic Ridge, where the North American and Eurasian tectonic plates hitch up . . . except they're splitsville – at the rate of 2.5 millimetres a year. That's right, I'm slowly being pulled apart by continental drift. My geology suffers the occasional temper tantrum, due to its geysers, hot springs and volcanoes. In 2010, I gave most of Europe a piece of my mind and sent forth a cloud of volcanic ash that grounded airline flights across the continent. I'm not all about mayhem, though. The Althing, my parliament, was founded in 930c.e. – it's the world's oldest legislature. Sooo civilized!

Denmark
EUROPE

- Denmark's royal family has reigned uninterrupted for over 1000 years
- Pigs outnumber humans in Denmark, by as many as four to one

I have a playful streak: my country-people invented LEGO® and I'm home to the Tivoli Gardens, one of the world's oldest amusement parks. Among my most famous sons is Hans Christian Andersen – storyteller extraordinaire. Who hasn't read his moral tales of vain emperors, little mermaids and ugly ducklings?

Even my shape is whimsical: I'm a peninsula with an archipelago of 406 islands, and I'm surrounded by the North Sea, Baltic Sea, Kattegat Strait, Skagerrak Strait and (if you count my territories of Greenland and the Faroe Islands), the North Atlantic and Arctic. You'd need an Excel spreadsheet to keep track of my natural harbours. Nowhere am I less than 48 kilometres from the sea, and I have 11,770 kilometres of coastline. Oh yes, I love bridges: The Great Belt links my islands of Zealand and Funen, while the Øresund Link connects my capital to Malmö in Sweden. I'm even connected to Germany by bridge (and land, and – soon – underwater tunnel). Not bad for the smallest country in Scandinavia, eh?

SIZE:
43,094 sq km

POPULATION:
5,594,000

CURRENCY:
Danish krone

CAPITAL:
Copenhagen

LANGUAGE:
Danish

Norway

EUROPE

* Oslo's Viking ship museum features a real Viking ship excavated from a burial mound
* On average, Norway's children spend 16.9 years in school

I'm more than the naked eye can see. Specifically, the part of my landmass that unfurls under the sea – my continental shelf – is four times the size of my dry land. In the 1970s, geologists discovered vast deposits of natural gas and oil beneath my seabed. Thanks to that, my citizens enjoy free healthcare, free education and the highest standard of living in Scandinavia. My coastline is feathered by hundreds of islands, islets and bays. No surprise, then, that I am rich in fish and support the largest fishing industry in Europe.

Ancient glaciers carved a landscape of fjords ringed by craggy cliffs. It must be all the *lutefisk* (codfish soaked in lye) and lingonberries they eat, but my people have exploration in their bones. Ever since the Vikings, they've been known for it. In 1911, Norwegian explorer Roald Amundsen led the first expedition to the South Pole, and Fridtjof Nansen was the first person to sail across the Arctic Ocean. *Tusen takk* ("Thanks!"), guys, you make me proud!

SIZE:
323,802 sq km

POPULATION:
5,265,000

CURRENCY:
Norwegian krone

CAPITAL:
Oslo

LANGUAGE:
Norwegian

Sweden

EUROPE

- Sweden's Riksbank, founded in 1668, is the world's oldest national bank
- At August's crayfish festivals, the crustaceans are cooked in beer and topped with dill

Bursting with natural resources, much of my land is forest, and logging accounts for at least 10 per cent of all my industry. I'm steeped in minerals, too. Four elements in the periodic table take their names from just one village, Ytterby: erbium, terbium, yttrium and ytterbium. I'm especially rich in uranium, which is used as a fuel in nuclear power plants. But I have a conscience: I tax nuclear power, subsidize wind power and was the first country to establish an Environmental Protection Agency. Alfred Nobel showed similar concern. This native of Stockholm invented dynamite, but wanted to leave a less explosive legacy, so endowed the Nobel Prizes for excellence in the arts and sciences.

Anyone fancy a *semla*? My national treat, these wheat buns are stuffed with almond paste and cream. And kids, if you snatch one rudely from the plate, you won't get your hand slapped. In 1979, I outlawed corporal punishment, leading the world in this humane legislation!

- **SIZE:**
  450,295 sq km
- **POPULATION:**
  9,880,000
- **CURRENCY:**
  Swedish krona
- **CAPITAL:**
  Stockholm
- **LANGUAGE:**
  Swedish

Finland

EUROPE

☀ Watch the northern lights in Lapland from the comfort of a heated glass igloo

☀ Finns love to take a sauna – a type of steam bath – it's their way of life

I am Europe's most sparsely populated country and share my northern Lapland region with Norway and Sweden. It is named for the reindeer-herding Lapp, or Sami, our indigenous people. Inspired by my frozen landscape, Finnish composer Jean Sibelius (1865–1957) claimed his sixth symphony reminded him of the scent of the first snow. Head to my far north and you'll see how the "midnight" sun stays above the horizon from mid-May until July. In winter, the northern lights – splashes of pink, green, violet and yellow light – flash across my darkened skies. Known as the "aurora borealis", this show is created by solar particles smashing into the Earth's atmospheric gases. Sami legend holds that whistling to the lights brings bad luck, lest they swoop down and spirit you away.

I may sound primitive but, trust me, I most definitely am not! My capital Helsinki, known as the Pearl of the Baltic, is home to the textile factory in which the bold and colourful Marimekko fabrics come to life.

○ **SIZE:**
338,145 sq km

◐ **POPULATION:**
5,498,000

○ **CURRENCY:**
Euro

● **CAPITAL:**
Helsinki

○ **LANGUAGES:**
Finnish, Swedish

Republic of Ireland

EUROPE

- ✷ Ireland became a republic in 1949, when it severed its ties with the United Kingdom
- ✷ Dublin's O'Connell Bridge over the Liffey River is as wide as it is long

True, I'm known as the Emerald Isle, but don't get your hopes up. There are no caverns of precious jewels here. (Don't expect to find any leprechauns, either, with their tiny pots of gold!) No, my intense green hue – visible even in satellite images – is due to grass: more than 80 per cent of me is covered with the stuff. Whether wild or cultivated, it thrives due to the moderating climate influence of the North Atlantic Current, a branch of the Gulf Stream. Grazing animals stay on my rich pastures for nearly 300 days a year; the intense yellow of Irish butter is due to the cows' natural diet.

Boy does it rain here – as much as 100 centimetres fall in the east per year and 140 centimetres in the west. And would you believe that I'm Europe's second-least forested country (after Iceland)? No one knows why exactly, but by the end of the 19th century, the broadleaf forest that once covered me had disappeared. Most likely, my people simply cut it all down for fuel, homes and ships.

○ **SIZE:**
70,273 sq km

◉ **POPULATION:**
4,952,000

○ **CURRENCY:**
Euro

◉ **CAPITAL:**
Dublin

○ **LANGUAGES:**
English, Gaelic

United Kingdom

EUROPE

* The clocktower at London's Westminster Palace is Elizabeth Tower; its bell is "Big Ben"
* In 2016, U.K. citizens voted for "Brexit" – a withdrawal from the European Union
* All horses, donkeys, and ponies living in the U.K. must have a passport

Watch me evolve. I've been tramped across by lots of people: Picts, Celts, Romans, Anglo Saxons . . . Many have left their mark, from Stonehenge in my south to Hadrian's Wall in my north. My government has changed from an absolute monarchy in Tudor times to a constitutional monarchy, with a head of state (my fab queen) and a prime minister heading a democratically elected parliament. I've suffered (the bubonic plague, the Great Fire of London, the Blitz), but I was once head of the largest empire ever known. Today, 14 overseas territories remain within my jurisdiction and I am one of the world's biggest donors of foreign aid.

So what's my secret? (Not my cuisine . . . others sneer at the way I overcook vegetables.) Maybe it's my mild climate? Influenced by the North Atlantic Current, it is perfect for farming – almost 70 per cent of my land is agricultural. Or perhaps it's my gentle geography – stunning hill-climbing highlands to the north and rolling lowlands to the south? Some might even say my good fortune is down to my people. I've known charismatic rulers (Elizabeth I, Winston Churchill) and artists to die for (William Shakespeare, The Beatles). What's more, today, my population represents over 60 ethnic groups and every major religion.

- **SIZE:**
  243,610 sq km
- **POPULATION:**
  64,430,000
- **CURRENCY:**
  British pound sterling
- **CAPITAL:**
  London
- **LANGUAGE:**
  English

From Mainland to Island

Around 18,000 years ago, the U.K. was attached to the north-western edge of Europe. Around 6000 B.C.E., three huge landslides beneath the sea created a tsunami that ripped the land from the continent.

Four in One

The United Kingdom is made up of four nations. Besides England, the nations and their respective capitals are: Scotland (Edinburgh), Wales (Cardiff) and Northern Ireland (Belfast). Once governed solely from London, each nation has been legally given certain governing powers in recent years.

Spain

EUROPE

- ✳ The spires of Antoni Gaudí's Sagrada Família dominate the Barcelona skyline
- ✳ Andalusia, in the south, is home to a form of song, dance and music called "flamenco"

I occupy most of the Iberian Peninsula, an ancient name that refers to my Ebro River. After climbing the Pyrenees on my northern border with France or the Sierra Nevada mountains that protect my southern reaches, kick back on the Meseta – the high central plateau that dominates my interior.

If a country were a recipe, I'd be the exotic one with a list of distinct flavours. To my north is the Basque country, where a very proud nation has sought independence from Spain in recent years. Then there are the Catalans. Centered around vibrant Barcelona in my north-east, these guys consider themselves a separate nation already. My Alhambra Palace in Granada was built by the Moors, who arrived from North Africa in the sixth century. Thanks to my climate, I have a wealth of sun-blessed fruits and vegetables to throw into the pot: oranges, mangoes, grapes, tomatoes and onions. And where the Mediterranean meets the Atlantic, my seas are full of red mullet, tuna and octopus.

- ○ **SIZE:**
  505,370 sq km
- ○ **POPULATION:**
  48,563,000
- ○ **CURRENCY:**
  Euro
- ● **CAPITAL:**
  Madrid
- ○ **LANGUAGE:**
  Spanish

Portugal

* Portugal's largest river, the Tagus, flows west from Spain and is 1007 kilometres long
* Glazed ceramic tiles introduced by the Moors decorate many façades and interiors

Sometimes I'm tempted to slip my moorings off the edge of the Iberian Peninsula and sail away into the Atlantic. Who knows what I'd discover? After all, my Prince Henry the Navigator is said to have kickstarted the Age of Discovery with his maritime endeavors of the 1400s. Swashbucklers Vasco da Gama and Ferdinand Magellan soon followed. These men put wind in the sails of Europe's rush toward colonization and gained major riches for me! And what better sight to behold on returning home, than the iconic Belém Tower rising from my Lisbon shores.

With 800 kilometres of coastline along the Atlantic Ocean, not to mention my two archipelagos (take a bow – Madeira and the Azores), it's little wonder I'm so drawn to the sea. Just look at my exports – one-fifth of them are fish, such as sardines and tuna. In fact, I am a fan of water all round: My mountainous north sees as much as five times the rain that falls in my low-lying south.

○ **SIZE:**
92,090 sq km

◉ **POPULATION:**
10,834,000

○ **CURRENCY:**
Euro

◉ **CAPITAL:**
Lisbon

○ **LANGUAGE:**
Portuguese

Andorra

EUROPE

So, I resemble a cute belly button nestling in the mountainous midriff between Spain and France – don't laugh! I've been around since 1278, when a charter was signed establishing my sovereignty. I'm so mountainous that almost all of my buildings sit in valleys – even the Casa de la Vall, home to my General Council. Mountains have an upside, though – my Grandvalira ski resort is one of the most popular in the Pyrenees.

- ○ **SIZE:** 468 sq km
- ◐ **POPULATION:** 86,000
- ○ **CURRENCY:** Euro
- ● **CAPITAL:** Andorra la Vella
- ○ **LANGUAGE:** Catalan

Monaco

EUROPE

A principality on the French Riviera, I am ruled by the Grimaldi dynasty; they live in the Prince's Palace, a stronghold since 1297. I've got a coastline you can conquer in a jog: 4 kilometres and, boy, what a coastline (yachts galore). I'm all about risk: My casino in Monte Carlo attracts some of the world's richest high rollers, and my Grand Prix is run through my cliff-lined streets instead of on a track!

- ○ **SIZE:** 2 sq km
- ◐ **POPULATION:** 31,000
- ○ **CURRENCY:** Euro
- ● **CAPITAL:** Monaco
- ○ **LANGUAGE:** French

Liechtenstein

EUROPE

* Of Liechtenstein's five medieval-era castles, three are ruins and one is a museum
* The last of the five castles – Vaduz Castle – is the king's home

At only 161 square kilometres, I may be the world's sixth-smallest country, but I offer plenty to sink your teeth into. In fact, check out your grandma's teeth (ask politely)! They were probably made here; I'm the world's largest supplier of dentures.

Wedged in tight between Switzerland and Austria, I get no respect from beach bums: I'm one of only two double-landlocked countries in the world. But another kind of bum – ski bums – love me. You see, about half my land is Alpine mountains. These handsome peaks originated millions of years ago in ancient Africa, would you believe, the result of tremendous tectonic forces beneath the Earth's crust. Today, their forests teem with wildlife – deer, marmots, hazel grouse, foxes and stoats. My mountains are heavily regulated to protect against erosion and preserve the ecology of those fine slopes. Oh, and those skiers? They aren't true bums: they've snagged an impressive 11 Olympic medals in Alpine skiing.

○ **SIZE:**
161 sq km

◉ **POPULATION:**
38,000

○ **CURRENCY:**
Swiss franc

◉ **CAPITAL:**
Vaduz

○ **LANGUAGE:**
German

59

France

EUROPE

- The world's first hot-air balloon was created in France by the Montgolfier brothers (1783)
- The island of Mont St. Michel is joined to France's north-east coast via a bridge
- Paris is famous for its Eiffel Tower and the cathedral of Notre-Dame

*S*acrebleu! I've been through many difficulties to become the *magnifique* country I am today. I've endured invaders, such as Julius Caesar (he took over when I was known as Gaul), and the whims of the Sun King, Louis XIV, with his thing for mirrors (there are 357 of them in just one hall at the Palace of Versailles). I suffered a revolution featuring guillotines, and cruel trench warfare during World War I that took a million and a half of my people's lives.

Still, I have panache (that's style to you): good bread, cheese, wine and a perfectly tilted beret help ease the pain. The United Nations awarded my culinary traditions status as a world cultural icon! It's true, I am devoted to products that promote *joie de vivre*: my fertile fields grow the fine things in life, such as grapes for my lovely bubbly champagne. In sunny southern Provence, I grow field after field of fragrant lavender. I cultivate jasmine for the world-famous French perfume Chanel No. 5. Just one bottle contains 1000 French jasmine buds! Besides my fertile agricultural fields, I am also known for my mountain ranges, of which I have four: the Vosges, Jura, Pyrenees and, of course, the Alps, site of the first Winter Olympics in the ski resort of Chamonix.

○ **SIZE:**
643,801 sq km

◉ **POPULATION:**
62,814,000

○ **CURRENCY:**
Euro

◉ **CAPITAL:**
Paris

○ **LANGUAGE:**
French

Ascend the Podium, *ma Mère!*
The French government awards mothers with many children the Medal of the French Family: Bronze for six children, silver for seven and if you can go the distance with eight, Mum (*mère*) takes the gold.

Overseas Territories

France's territories include Guadeloupe and Martinique in the Caribbean, French Guiana in South America and Réunion and Mayotte in the Indian Ocean. Designated "overseas departments", their people have the same rights as those in regions of mainland France.

Netherlands

EUROPE

☀ Keukenhof, in the town of Lisse, is home to the world's best-known tulip festival
☀ The Dutch women's field hockey team has won the World Cup a record seven times

Go with the flow? No way. Flooding is not my thing. In the contest between the Netherlands and the North Sea, it's advantage Netherlands. In 1953, a storm breached aging dikes and killed 1800 people, so I got serious about flood control. Today, I deploy canals, dikes, artificial dunes planted with grass to create dense, absorbent mats and enormous floating gates that close when tides surge. Otherwise, I'd be drowned, because almost half my land is below sea level.

My water-wrangling smarts mean that my population prospers. After the U.S., I am the second-largest exporter of agricultural products in the world – flowers, meat, dairy – and grow one-quarter of all the vegetables exported from Europe. Did you know that my Amsterdam airport and Rotterdam seaport are among the world's busiest today? Well, I've had trade in my bones for centuries, peaking with the establishment of the Dutch East India Company in the 1600s.

○ **SIZE:**
41,543 sq km

◉ **POPULATION:**
17,017,000

○ **CURRENCY:**
Euro

● **CAPITAL:**
Amsterdam

○ **LANGUAGE:**
Dutch

Belgium

EUROPE

A convenient rendezvous point for some of the bloodiest battles of two world wars, is it any wonder I've made diplomacy my business? My capital, Brussels, is home to the headquarters of NATO and the EU. My people get testy at times, with deep divisions between my southern Walloons and my northern Flemings. But my most serious debate is with France, and whether or not French fries are, in fact, Belgian. They are!

- **SIZE:** 30,528 sq km
- **POPULATION:** 11,409,000
- **CURRENCY:** Euro
- **CAPITAL:** Brussels
- **LANGUAGES:** Dutch, French, German

Luxembourg

EUROPE

I originated as a fortress and castle built on a strategic promontory known as the Bock, which stands inside a loop of the Alzette River. Views from the top look out over my lush Bon Pays region. I grew outward from the castle, while the castle grew deep into the ground; over 11 miles (17.5 km) of tunnels remain today! In World War II, General George Patton liberated me from German occupation in the Battle of the Bulge, and today I am his burial ground.

- **SIZE:** 2586 sq km
- **POPULATION:** 582,000
- **CURRENCY:** Euro
- **CAPITAL:** Luxembourg City
- **LANGUAGES:** Luxembourgish, French, German

Switzerland

EUROPE

- ☀ Switzerland is famous for chocolate, cheese, luxury watches and ski resorts
- ☀ At 101 metres high, Bern's cathedral spire is the tallest in Switzerland

○ **SIZE:**
41,277 sq km

◉ **POPULATION:**
8,179,000

○ **CURRENCY:**
Euro

● **CAPITAL:**
Bern

○ **LANGUAGES:**
German, French, Italian,
Romansch

Landlocked, I have a landscape dominated by the Swiss Alps and the Jura Mountains. My Alps are home to the Cresta Run skeleton bobsled track at St. Moritz and Europe's highest train station, 4158 metres, up at Jungfrau peak. Between the mountain ranges, my Swiss plateau is home to two major cities, Geneva and Zurich. And I still have room for more than 1500 lakes – Geneva and Constance are two of Europe's largest.

I'm neutral, but that doesn't mean I'm boring. You see, after the Napoleonic Wars (when I was invaded by France, in 1798), my European neighbours saw my potential as a military buffer zone. In 1815, I was declared "perpetually neutral". I am also proud of the moment that Swiss John-Henri Dunant founded the Red Cross, an organization that protects victims of conflict. His idea won him the first Nobel Peace Prize, in 1901.

Austria

* The Austrian city of Innsbruck has hosted the Winter Olympics twice
* The Danube, Europe's second-longest river, crosses Austria from east to west

SIZE:
83,871 sq km

POPULATION:
8,712,000

CURRENCY:
Euro

CAPITAL:
Vienna

LANGUAGE:
German

Shall we dance? The Viennese Waltz, of course! My waltz is just one of the traditions I'm famed for, as are competitive cowbell ringing and yodelling – important skills if you're a cowherd trying to call in the cows or communicate with a pal living across the valley. You see, about two-thirds of my land is Alpine mountains, and one-third of my people live in the valleys. In the olden days before texting, yodelling was a great way to make a date to meet for Wiener Schnitzel (my traditional dish, a breaded veal cutlet).

Still, I'm so much more than yodelling cow herders. The Staatsoper (State Opera House) in Vienna is fabled for its elaborate shows. And if you love pastry, you might never want to leave; my coffee houses offer the richest *tortes* around, such as my jam-filled Linzer Torte, the world's oldest cake.

Italy

EUROPE

* Landmarks include Brunelleschi's Dome in Florence and Rome's Colosseum
* The "ball" that Italy's "boot" is kicking is the island of Sicily

I'm one country that's hard to contain. If my innards aren't rumbling (I sit on a fault line between the African and Eurasian tectonic plates, so I'm highly prone to earthquakes), they're spewing – I'm home to Europe's three active volcanoes: Etna, Stromboli and Vesuvius. And don't hate me for being beautiful! I may be shaped like an old boot, but there is nothing inelegant or down-at-heel about me. I'm overflowing with art, such as Michelangelo's statue of David and Canaletto's paintings of Venetian canals (gondolas, and all). My ancient monuments, the Roman Forum and the Trevi Fountain, are fabled for their beauty, but don't forget my earthier marvels of the past: The Cloaca Maxima, or great sewer, dates from 6 B.C.E. and channels Roman wastewater to this day.

It may also give you a jolt to know that I can claim Alessandro Volta as a native son. He was the scientist who invented the first battery by analysing twitching frog legs. (It's a galvanizing story.)

- **SIZE:**
  301,340 sq km
- **POPULATION:**
  62,008,000
- **CURRENCY:**
  Euro
- **CAPITAL:**
  Rome
- **LANGUAGE:**
  Italian

San Marino

EUROPE

Buried inside Italy, I've been sitting pretty atop Mount Titano in the Apennine Mountains since 301 C.E., when Marinus, a Croatian stonecutter, founded a monastery. I'm one of the world's oldest states! Today, you can visit my three medieval fortresses with superb Adriatic vistas and contemplate the artifacts in my Museum of Torture. You'll need a strong stomach; they have a knee-breaker, a traction bench and an iron maiden.

- ○ **SIZE:** 61 sq km
- ◉ **POPULATION:** 33,000
- ○ **CURRENCY:** Euro
- ● **CAPITAL:** City of San Marino
- ○ **LANGUAGE:** Italian

Vatican City

EUROPE

Holier than thou? You bet I am! A walled enclave in Rome, I'm divinely tiny, the world's smallest sovereign state. I boast some highly connected residents (the Pope, not to name drop). St. Peter's Basilica, where the Pope celebrates mass, is built over the tombs of medieval popes and the apostle Peter. And while my Swiss Guards may look harmless in their striped pantaloons, don't cross them; they are expert marksmen!

- ○ **SIZE:** 0.44 sq km
- ◉ **POPULATION:** 1000
- ○ **CURRENCY:** Euro
- ● **CAPITAL:** Vatican City
- ○ **LANGUAGE:** Italian

Germany

EUROPE

- ❋ Berlin's Zoologischer Garten is the world's largest zoo: 0.34 square kilometres
- ❋ The Brandenburg Gate, in Berlin, is the site of many historical events
- ❋ Skyscraper-filled Frankfurt is home to the European Central Bank

Don't be afraid – come in under the dark evergreen canopy of my Schwarzwald, or Black Forest. It's nothing sinister – black just refers to the dark shadows created by the conifers. On second thoughts, perhaps you should be cautious. After all, my Brothers Grimm (again, don't let the name spook you) are world-famous for their folk stories of child-eating witches living in tempting candy cottages and ravenous wolves nestled deep in Grandma's feather bed. And if fairy tales are your thing, don't forget to pass by Lorelei, the murmuring rock in the middle of my Rhine River, where a fabled golden-haired siren has caused many a shipwreck.

If, as you journey through my land, you think you hear music, it could be the ghosts of my composers, who practically invented classical music: Bach, Beethoven, Brahms . . . I could go on. Their chords reach to the rafters of my imposing cathedrals, such as Cologne (it took 632 years to build and can hold 40,000 people) or Freiburg, with its 44-stop organ that Mozart himself praised. Life in modern Germany is prosperous: my export economy is the world's largest – bigger even than China's. As in many developed countries, though, the population is declining, and from 1989 to 2009, 2000 German schools were closed because there were not enough children!

- ○ **SIZE:**
  357,022 sq km
- ◉ **POPULATION:**
  80,723,000
- ○ **CURRENCY:**
  Euro
- ● **CAPITAL:**
  Berlin
- ○ **LANGUAGE:**
  German

Prize Pickles

The gherkins of Germany's Spreewald region are so crunchy and spicy that they are protected by the European Union. They boast their own cuke-friendly bicycle route known in English as the Pickle Path.

Shifting Borders

Before Germany became a nation-state, in 1871, the region had been a collection of small, mostly German-speaking states. In 1949, following World War II, the country was divided once more – into East and West (even Berlin was divided by the Berlin Wall). The two halves were reunited in 1990.

Poland

EUROPE

* Polish Marie Curie was the first woman to win a Nobel Prize (for discovering radium)
* *Pysanky*, or decorated Easter eggs, are a traditional Polish craft

○ **SIZE:**
3071 sq km

◉ **POPULATION:**
38,523,000

○ **CURRENCY:**
Polish zloty

● **CAPITAL:**
Warsaw

○ **LANGUAGE:**
Polish

You would need time-lapse photography to keep track of my shifting borders over the years. In 1492, I was the largest territory in Europe, but by 1795, Russia, Prussia and Austria had all but gobbled me up. I didn't exist again as a country until the end of World War I.

Oh, but what a fine country, with super tall Tatras Mountains on my border with Slovakia and the stunning Masurian Lake District in my north-eastern corner. My longest river, the Vistula, winds its way from north to south, cutting me in half. My Palace of Culture and Science in Warsaw is the eighth-tallest building in Europe, while Gdańsk is one of the busiest ports on the Baltic Sea. My Wieliczka Salt Mine near Krakow has existed since the 13th century and boasts an underground salt cathedral and three chandeliers of crystallized rock salt.

Estonia

EUROPE

Located between the Baltic Sea and the Gulf of Finland, I'm a flat, forested land of equal parts tradition and innovation. While the warrior hero of my national epic poem, *Kalevipoeg*, took battle advice from a hedgehog, more recently my people helped invent Skype. Chorale singing is a favourite pastime, a way to establish unity and express national pride as we twice (in 1918 and 1991) fought for independence from the Soviet Union.

- ○ **SIZE:** 45,228 sq km
- ◉ **POPULATION:** 1,259,000
- ○ **CURRENCY:** Euro
- ● **CAPITAL:** Tallinn
- ○ **LANGUAGE:** Estonian

Latvia

EUROPE

Situated on the northern Baltic Sea, but with ice-free ports, I'm a land of forests, bogs, 12,000 rivers and 3000 little lakes. I'm good for what ails you! I offer remedies from the woods: my national liqueur is brewed from 24 plants, buds, juices, roots, plant oils and berries. Following occupations by Germany, Poland, Sweden and the Soviet Union, events that led to my independence in 1991 are known as the Singing Revolution.

- ○ **SIZE:** 64,589 sq km
- ◉ **POPULATION:** 1,966,000
- ○ **CURRENCY:** Euro
- ● **CAPITAL:** Riga
- ○ **LANGUAGES:** Latvian, Russian

Lithuania

EUROPE

Exposed on the Baltic Sea, I've been invaded by Russia, Sweden and Germany among others. No wonder, then, that my national symbol is Vytis, a white knight mounted on a rearing stallion, brandishing his broadsword. Having gained independence from the Soviet Union in 1991, I still have many Soviet-era buildings – apartment blocks and a super-skinny TV tower. But my capital also has one of Europe's largest old-town districts.

○ **SIZE:**
65,300 sq km

○ **POPULATION:** 2,854,000   ● **CAPITAL:** Vilnius

○ **CURRENCY:** Euro   ○ **LANGUAGE:** Lithuanian

Slovakia

EUROPE

I split from the Czechs in 1993 and I'm so proud! The name of my capital, Bratislava, is just a big brag: it combines root words for "brotherhood" and "glory". My High Tatras Mountains are the tallest in central Europe and offer killer ski resorts. I'm also cave central. My karst (eroded limestone) region has 712 caves – sometimes used for aging wine. The Dobsinská Ice Cave is superchilled: its temperature never rises above zero.

○ **SIZE:**
49,035 sq km

○ **POPULATION:** 5,446,000   ● **CAPITAL:** Bratislava

○ **CURRENCY:** Euro   ○ **LANGUAGE:** Slovak

Czech Republic

EUROPE

* The Czech Republic has more than 2000 castles, castle ruins and keeps
* Prague's 15th-century Charles Bridge has more than 30 statues of Christian saints

- **SIZE:**
  78,867 sq km
- **POPULATION:**
  10,645,000
- **CURRENCY:**
  Czech koruna
- **CAPITAL:**
  Prague
- **LANGUAGE:**
  Czech

A landlocked middleman, I have three main regions, Bohemia, Moravia and Silesia. My people are watched over by St. Vitus, who is said to protect against lightning, dog bites and oversleeping. My approachable terrain – gently rolling hills and low forested mountains – means that, for centuries, I've been a friendly travel route for traders, funneling them along the Amber Road, an ancient trade route between the Baltic and Mediterranean Seas. My Vltava River slices my capital in two as it journeys 435 kilometres across my land.

Recent history? Well, Slovakia and I were once a single country (Czechoslovakia) under Communist control. In 1989, our people staged a revolution to set us free. Then Slovakia and I decided to go our separate ways in 1993. Today, I like to call myself Czechia for short.

Hungary

EUROPE

- Budapest's parliament building sits on the banks of the Danube River
- Relaxing in Budapest's thermal baths is a way of life for some

SIZE:
93,028 sq km

POPULATION:
9,875,000

CURRENCY:
Hungarian forint

CAPITAL:
Budapest

LANGUAGE:
Hungarian

Flat to rolling plains are the hallmark of my land, divided by the Danube River flowing north to south on its way to the Black Sea. And no, I'm not *hungry*, thank you. We eat well here – ever heard of Hungarian goulash? The Hungarian word for it, *gulyásleves*, means "herdsmen's soup" – cooked by the cowboys!

Hungaria was a medieval name for me, but I also call my people Magyars, for the warrior tribe that roamed me in the ninth century. Love those guys – led by their Grand Prince, Arpád, they migrated across the Carpathian Mountains to conquer and settle my land.

I was worth grabbing; I'm home to Europe's largest thermal lake, Hévíz. Situated on an ancient peat bed, its waters are said to be medicinal! I also boast Europe's largest natural grasslands – the Puszta.

Romania

EUROPE

* Romania's Statue of Decebalus, in Orsova, is Europe's largest rock sculpture
* Timisoara was the first European city to have electric street lights (1884)

I boast a stretch of Black Sea coastline fed by the great Danube River. My Danube Delta, Europe's second-longest river delta, is made up of an intricate network of marshes, lagoons and streamlets. They provide secluded habitats for endangered birds, such as the Dalmatian pelican and great cormorant. But let's face it: people know me best for my forbidding Carpathian Mountains, home to Europe's highest concentration of brown bears, wolves and lynxes. The range cuts a path across me from north to south-west. And don't forget my castles – I have at least ten – or the Palace of Parliament in my capital, Bucharest. It happens to be the world's second-largest administrative building after the Pentagon in Washington, D.C.

Back to my castles, though, and the ruin of Poenari Castle, in particular. Looming in grim isolation on one of my Carpathian peaks, it's one of the many rumored haunts of Vlad the Impaler. Yes, Count Dracula – my favourite son!

○ **SIZE:**
238,391 sq km

◑ **POPULATION:**
21,600,000

○ **CURRENCY:**
Romanian leu

● **CAPITAL:**
Bucharest

○ **LANGUAGE:**
Romanian

Serbia

EUROPE

☀ Serbia's capital, Belgrade, sits at the point at which the Danube and Sava rivers meet

☀ Wolves roam the Deliblato Sands desert to the north of the country

Take my word for it: I'm tough. I need to be – the Balkan peninsula, my home, has been ravaged by conflict for centuries, as my neighbours and I have fought for our independence. First we battled against the Ottoman Empire and then against each other! My rugged topography matches my reputation: the Dinaric Alps slash through my south-west; to the east, the Balkan Mountains warn off Romania and Bulgaria. At least my climate isn't fearsome: continental in the north and Adriatic in the south, it's ideal for growing fruit. I export tonnes of delicious raspberries, plums and apples.

Culturally, I am buzzing with a wealth of national crafts and traditions: kilim-rug weaving thrives in my south-eastern city of Pirot, while Kovačica, in the Vojvodina region to my north, is a centre for a "naïve" style of folk-art painting. My lively country dances include the *kolo*, in which people clasp arms to dance in a circle, and the *lesa*, which involves two parallel lines of linked dancers.

○ **SIZE:**
77,474 sq km

◉ **POPULATION:**
7,144,000

○ **CURRENCY:**
Serbian dinar

● **CAPITAL:**
Belgrade

○ **LANGUAGE:**
Serbian

Slovenia

EUROPE

Alpine mountains dominate my north, while caves and underground rivers riddle my south. Head east and you'll find fertile land, good for growing wheat. It's miniature, but I even boast a coastline on the Adriatic Sea. My heritage is Slavic, but I'm geographically close to Italy: Venice lies just across the water. I have a passion for the art of puppetry and Ljubljana, my capital, hosts a famed Puppet Theatre and Museum.

- **SIZE:** 20,273 sq km
- **POPULATION:** 1,978,000
- **CURRENCY:** Euro
- **CAPITAL:** Ljubljana
- **LANGUAGE:** Slovene

Montenegro

EUROPE

I stuck with Serbia when the rest of Yugoslavia went bye-bye in 2003. But in 2006, I voted to go my own way. Check out my mountain gorges, monasteries and mausoleums – what's not to like? Don't pet my feral cats. My medieval city Kotor, is kitty central! Its Cats Museum features a complete cluster of catty exhibits. And on my Mogren Beach near Budva, a statue of a woman confronts the waves in an awesome ballet pose!

- **SIZE:** 13,812 sq km
- **POPULATION:** 645,000
- **CURRENCY:** Euro
- **CAPITAL:** Podgorica
- **LANGUAGES:** Serbian, Montenegrin

Croatia

EUROPE

- An equestrian statue of military hero Josip Jelacic stands in a square in the capital
- The spotted Dalmatian dog originated in the Dalmatia region of Croatia

Just across the Adriatic Sea from Italy, I'm shaped like an irregular pair of tweezers with a 1800-kilometre coastline and the handle of the Istrian peninsula jutting into the sea to my north. My rural fields are dotted with *kazun* – stone shelters with conical roofs that were used for storage and shelter for olive-grove workers during the days of the Roman Empire.

At my southern tip, thick stone walls that date from the ninth century encircle my ancient city of Dubrovnik, and are topped with forts. And how many modern city centres get built in the middle of a palace? Split, on my Istrian peninsula, is just that: hip restaurants, shops and homes sit within and around the Emperor Diocletian's Palace, dating from 295 c.e. Some of the white limestone used to construct that palace came from my island of Brac. The White House in Washington, D.C. is built with the same glittering white stone. Little wonder I'm known as the pearl of the Adriatic!

○ **SIZE:** 56,594 sq km		● **CAPITAL:** Zagreb	
● **POPULATION:** 4,314,000		○ **LANGUAGE:** Croatian	
○ **CURRENCY:** Croatian kuna			

Bosnia & Herzegovina

EUROPE

* The capital, Sarajevo, was the first European city to have an electric tram
* Sarajevo's modern skyline is pierced by the Avaz Twist Tower, with a twisted façade

○ **SIZE:**
51,197 sq km

◉ **POPULATION:**
3,862,000

○ **CURRENCY:**
Bosnian convertible marka

● **CAPITAL:**
Sarajevo

○ **LANGUAGES:** Bosnian, Serbian, Croatian

My double name links the names of my two regions: northern Bosnia and southern Herzegovina. My landscape is dominated by the Dinaric Alps, primeval forests and many rivers, including the Neretva in Mostar, famed for its emerald colour. My karst plateau near Montenegro in the south features a limestone terrain riddled with caves and potholes. At least seven waterfalls scattered in my mountains boast multiple cascades. Splash!

I'm also rich in mineral ores; horseshoes were once an export and my traditional handicrafts include engraved metalwork.

Ottoman ruler Suleiman the Magnificent ordered the building of the iconic Starí Most Bridge in the city of Mostar, during the 16th century. Destroyed by shelling in the Croat-Bosniak War (1992–1994), its reincarnation uses some of the original pale stone.

Macedonia

EUROPE

I'm a landlocked region of mountains and lakes on the northern border of Greece. Poor but proud, I have recently splashed out on a new dome for my parliament. My Lake Ohrid is one of the world's oldest and deepest. It's a squishy-stuff museum, with snails and sponges found nowhere else on the Earth. And I must be doing something right: I'm the only former Yugoslav republic to achieve independence without bloodshed.

○ **SIZE:** 25,713 sq km

● **POPULATION:** 2,100,000   ● **CAPITAL:** Skopje

○ **CURRENCY:** Macedonian denar   ○ **LANGUAGE:** Macedonian

Albania

EUROPE

A small mountainous country, my long Adriatic coastline sports untouristy beaches. Inland, my lush fertile plains provide top spots for agriculture. I'm not a rich country; perhaps that inspired my revered native saint, Mother Teresa. Dotted around my landscape are 750,000 concrete bunkers – a legacy from my Communist past – now painted in bright colours and used as shelters for the homeless and as food kiosks!

○ **SIZE:** 28,748 sq km

● **POPULATION:** 3,039,000

○ **CURRENCY:** Albanian lek

● **CAPITAL:** Tirana

○ **LANGUAGE:** Albanian

Bulgaria
EUROPE

* Bulgaria's Rose Valley is the world's largest producer of rose oil for perfume
* Thick sheep's yogurt made in the mountains is some of the best in the world

○ **SIZE:**
110,879 sq km

◉ **POPULATION:**
7,145,000

○ **CURRENCY:**
Bulgarian lev

● **CAPITAL:**
Sofia

○ **LANGUAGE:**
Bulgarian

Founded in the seventh century, I'm one of Europe's oldest states. My people were Bulgars – semi-nomadic, equestrian warriors.

In my more recent history, I sided with the Axis powers (Germany, Italy and Japan) during World War II. Later, in the 1990s, I managed to shake off Soviet domination, and now I take pride in being a member of NATO and the EU.

A northern Danubian plain rolls inland from my coast on the Black Sea. In my south-west, you'll find the Rila and Rhodope mountains. Something super-healthy must be happening in those peaks and valleys because the region is home to the world's highest percentage of centenarians (people 100 years old, and over). My Kukeri festival sees dancers wearing furry hooded costumes cavorting through villages at dawn to ward off evil spirits.

Greece

EUROPE

* The Parthenon, a temple in Athens, honours the Greek goddess, Athena
* The island of Santorini is a caldera, the result of a volcanic eruption

Surrounded by four seas – the Aegean, Ionian, Cretan and Mediterranean – is it any wonder I count Odysseus, the adventurer who set sail from my Ionian isle, Ithaca, among my heroes? You'll find me at the tip of the Balkan peninsula plus a clutch of tiny islands (around 6000 – who's counting, only 227 are inhabited). Some call me the cradle of Western civilization. Sure, I'll take a bow.

I'm 80 per cent mountainous. You may have heard of my highest peak, Mount Olympus, where that old god Zeus lives. Don't confuse it with Olympia, though, site of the original Olympic Games – the two are hundreds of miles apart. My largest island, Crete, marks the southernmost limit of Europe. It served as the epicentre of Minoan civilization and dates back to 3000 B.C.E. Perhaps you think I make too much of my history, but all of my greatest assets have been around since that time. Honey, olive oil, wine and figs – all of them ancient and now major exports, along with natural sea sponges and Greek marble.

○ **SIZE:**
131,957 sq km

◕ **POPULATION:**
10,773,000

○ **CURRENCY:**
Euro

● **CAPITAL:**
Athens

○ **LANGUAGE:**
Greek

Cyprus

EUROPE

A beautiful island in the Mediterranean Sea, I'm cut in two by a UN-patrolled buffer zone. You see, my Turkish Cypriots have laid claim to my north from the rest of my Greek-dominated island. I'm skimmed by two mountain ranges north and south of a central plain. Near my city of Paphos, lie ancient ruins honouring Aphrodite, the Greek goddess of love. According to legend, she first touched land on my shore after rising from the sea on a scallop shell.

- **SIZE:** 9251 sq km
- **POPULATION:** 1,206,000
- **CURRENCY:** Euro
- **CAPITAL:** Nicosia
- **LANGUAGES:** Greek, Turkish

Malta

EUROPE

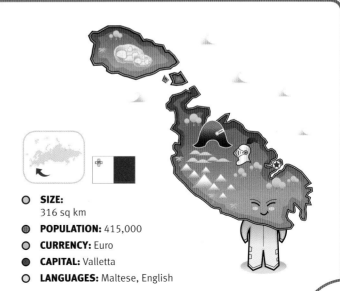

I was once connected to the ancient African super-continent; scientists have unearthed elephant fossils in my caves! Now I'm a Mediterranean island archipelago. Steep limestone cliffs with pretty coves and bays dominate my coastlines. In 1530, Emperor Charles V granted my sovereignty to the crusader Knights of St. John. Since then, I've been French and British, but I like being independent best of all!

- **SIZE:** 316 sq km
- **POPULATION:** 415,000
- **CURRENCY:** Euro
- **CAPITAL:** Valletta
- **LANGUAGES:** Maltese, English

Belarus

EUROPE

Landlocked, I consist mostly of lowlands with some stylish, flat-topped hills in my north-west – the Belarusian Ridge. In Vitebsk to the north-east, *zubr*, (that's European bison to you) roam the Berezinsky Biosphere Reserve. They are the continent's largest living mammal. If you think my capital's Gorky Park, established in 1800, seems old, think again. My Bialowieza Forest is primeval – from the earliest time in history.

- **SIZE:** 207,600 sq km
- **POPULATION:** 9,570,000
- **CURRENCY:** Belarusian ruble
- **CAPITAL:** Minsk
- **LANGUAGES:** Russian, Belarusian

Moldova

EUROPE

Tiny but spirited, I have rolling plains and super rich soils; both are ideal for growing crops for export – grains and beet in the north and grapes in the south. My Milestii Mici wine cellar rates as super cool. Created from an old limestone mine, its 200 kilometres of tunnels can be navigated by car or bus! Step into the forests that grow in my Dniester River floodplain and you might just spot a white-tailed sea eagle.

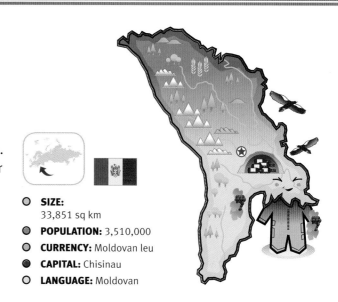

- **SIZE:** 33,851 sq km
- **POPULATION:** 3,510,000
- **CURRENCY:** Moldovan leu
- **CAPITAL:** Chisinau
- **LANGUAGE:** Moldovan

Ukraine

* Ukraine is one of Europe's largest grain exporters, a crucial breadbasket
* The world's worst nuclear energy accident occurred at Chernobyl, in Ukraine, in 1986

○ **SIZE:**
603,550 sq km

◉ **POPULATION:**
44,210,000

○ **CURRENCY:**
Ukrainian hryvnia

● **CAPITAL:**
Kiev

○ **LANGUAGE:**
Ukrainian

Situated north of the Black Sea in eastern Europe, I've been a prized land for many centuries and remain so – in recent years, Russia annexed my Crimean peninsula.

The Dnieper River, an ancient trade route on the Amber Road, flows through Kiev, my capital. In the 17th and 18th centuries, my people were Cossacks, daring horsemen and warriors of the steppes. These days, crops take up swathes of those Cossack lands; their rich, black soil is notoriously fertile. I'm big on seeds for oils – sunflower, hemp, poppy – and beets. Potatoes (I am one of Europe's largest exporters) grow farther north. Check out the primeval beech forests of my Carpathian Mountains or the ancient city of Chersonesus on the shores of the Black Sea – just two of my seven (that's right, seven) UNESCO World Heritage sites.

Russia

EUROPE

* The world's largest country by surface area – almost twice the size of the United States
* The Trans-Siberian Railway runs for 9298 kilometres from Moscow to Vladivostok
* The Hermitage Museum in St. Petersburg keeps around 70 cats on the lookout for rats

Modesty just isn't me, so I'll say it. I am *epic*. My vast land borders 14 other countries as well as the Arctic and Pacific Oceans, and I have oodles of amazements to boast about. For starters, temperatures in my Siberian tundra can dip as low as −50 degrees Celsius. My taiga in the Caucasus region is the world's largest forest and my Mount Elbrus, another Caucasian marvel, is Europe's highest mountain (not to brag, but it's also a volcano). If you're thirsty, there are plenty of refreshing sips in Lake Baikal, the world's oldest (25 million years) and largest freshwater lake. In 1957, my scientists launched *Sputnik I*, the Earth's first artificial satellite.

Ever seen a Matryoshka doll? These nesting figures, or "little matrons", were designed by the artist Sergey Malyutin in 1890, and are now popular all over the world. I'm also known for treasures of a more mineral kind. My Mirny Diamond Pit is one of the largest diamond mines in the world. Dig hard enough and you'll find gold, too.

For urban delights, head to Moscow, where the fancy, multicoloured onion domes of Saint Basil's Cathedral steal the show in Red Square. Or take in a show at the Bolshoi Ballet, scene of the *grand jeté* and the *demi-plié* for more than 200 years.

- **SIZE:**
  17,098,242 sq km
- **POPULATION:**
  142,355,000
- **CURRENCY:**
  Russian ruble
- **CAPITAL:**
  Moscow
- **LANGUAGE:**
  Russian

The Soviet Union

From 1922 until 1991, Russia was the largest and most powerful of 15 states that belonged to the Union of Soviet Socialist Republics. Moscow served as the union's capital and centre of government.

Two Continents

Russia is so vast that it spreads across two
continents – Europe and Asia – spanning eleven
time zones. The Asian region is by far the largest, yet
the majority of Russia's population lives in Europe.

Africa

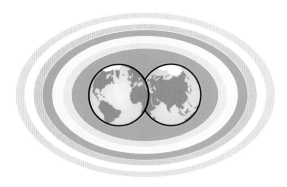

Are your senses up to a trial of strength? Just try to take me in. My Sahara, the world's hottest desert, is as big as the United States. My Serengeti savannah is full of pattern – see the rippling stripes of zebras as they canter across the plain, or the mosaic patches of an elegant giraffe's neck as it reaches to nibble from acacia treetops. In my Kalahari Desert, if you spot a crouched figure aiming a poison-tipped dart, it could be one of Namibia's Ju-Wasi bushmen. Possessors of some of the oldest *Homo sapiens* DNA, these people still live as hunter-gatherers well into the 21st century. How sharp is your ear? You may hear the rippling waters of my Nile, the world's longest river, stocked with grunting hippos and crocodiles, or the distant hum of great cities, such as Nairobi and Johannesburg.

* **Land mass:** 30,221,532 sq km
* **Number of countries:** 54
* **Biggest lake:** Victoria
* **Longest river:** Nile
* **Highest mountain:** Kilimanjaro

Africa

 Algeria

 Angola

 Benin

 Botswana

 Burkina Faso

 Burundi

 Cameroon

Cape Verde

 Central African Republic

 Chad

 Comoros

 Congo

 Congo, Democratic Republic of

 Djibouti

 Egypt

 Equatorial Guinea

 Eritrea

 Ethiopia

 Gabon

 Gambia, The

 Ghana

 Guinea

 Guinea-Bissau

 Ivory Coast

 Kenya

 Lesotho

 Liberia

 Libya

 Madagascar

 Malawi

 Mali

 Mauritania

 Mauritius

 Morocco

 Mozambique

 Namibia

 Niger

 Nigeria

Rwanda

São Tomé & Príncipe

 Senegal

Seychelles

 Sierra Leone

 Somalia

South Africa

 South Sudan

Sudan

 Swaziland

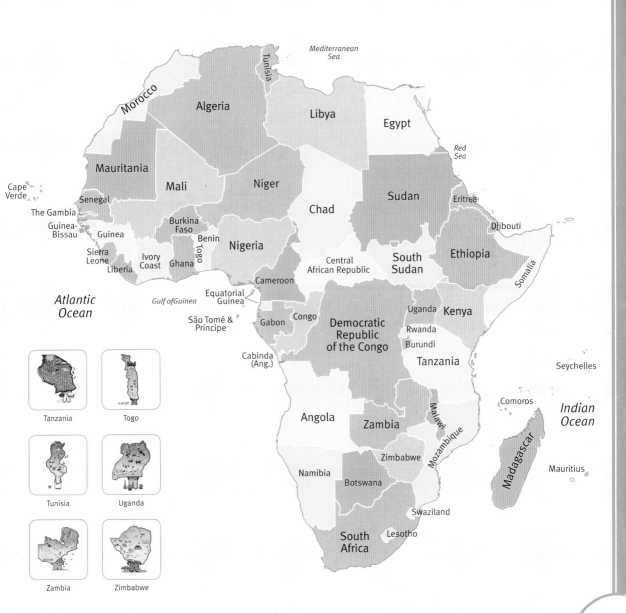

Mediterranean Sea

Morocco

Tunisia

Algeria

Libya

Egypt

Red Sea

Mauritania

Mali

Niger

Cape Verde

Senegal

The Gambia

Guinea-Bissau

Guinea

Sierra Leone

Liberia

Burkina Faso

Benin

Togo

Ivory Coast

Ghana

Chad

Nigeria

Sudan

Eritrea

Djibouti

Central African Republic

South Sudan

Ethiopia

Somalia

Cameroon

Gulf of Guinea

Equatorial Guinea

Atlantic Ocean

São Tomé & Príncipe

Gabon

Congo

Cabinda (Ang.)

Democratic Republic of the Congo

Uganda

Rwanda

Burundi

Kenya

Tanzania

Seychelles

Comoros

Indian Ocean

Angola

Zambia

Malawi

Mozambique

Madagascar

Mauritius

Zimbabwe

Namibia

Botswana

Swaziland

Lesotho

South Africa

Tanzania

Togo

Tunisia

Uganda

Zambia

Zimbabwe

Morocco

AFRICA

* Chefchaouen village is painted in shades of blue to mirror Morocco's cloudless sky
* Morocco annexed Western Sahara, a territory to the south, in the 1970s

A dual-aspect coastline, the scorching Sahara desert, and two mega mountain ranges – that's me in a nutshell. The Rif mountains border the Mediterranean to my north, while the Atlas Mountains cross me diagonally, north-east to south-west. My indigenous people, the Berbers, live in this rugged terrain. Their ancestors built ancient Marrakesh – a desert city fringed by palms and backed by towering snowy peaks.

In the Atlas foothills, the sweet scents of Persian roses and orange blossoms grown for the perfume trade linger in the air. Talking of scent, the richly ornamented, 14th-century Al-Attarine Madrasa (School of the Perfumers) fronts the perfume market in my medieval city of Fez. You'll see my signature decorative art there – mosaic tiling, or *zellige*. Throughout my land, *zellige* decorates the shady interior courtyard gardens that serve as the peaceful, private hearts of my traditional *riads*, or homes. There's no better place to enjoy my national drink – a glass of sweetened mint tea.

○ **SIZE:**
446,550 sq km

◉ **POPULATION:**
33,656,000

◉ **CURRENCY:**
Moroccan dirham

● **CAPITAL:**
Rabat

○ **LANGUAGES:**
Arabic, Berber

Algeria

☀ Algeria is situated in western North Africa, a region that was once called the Maghreb

☀ Algiers' *casbah* (citadel) once had 150 tiled public water fountains; six remain today

You'll need shades here: I'm famed for the intensity of my light and whitewashed, tumbledown buildings. Dusty desert siroccos blow west across me out to the Mediterranean, and the secluded little ports along my coast were for centuries the favourite haunts of Barbary pirates. In 1575, they captured Miguel de Cervantes, author of *Don Quixote*, and imprisoned him for five years.

The Atlas Mountains dominate my north and the Hoggar Mountains feature in my south, but most of my land is occupied by the scorching Sahara desert. The teensy fennec fox – the world's smallest – lives there and has huge, batlike ears that radiate heat. My coastal capital's *casbah* comprises a steeply pitched hilltop *medina* (village), a *souk* (marketplace) and densely packed houses that have existed since medieval times. The steepest street in the *casbah* has 472 steps. Also on the coast, my city Tipaza contains the ruins of a Roman military outpost with baths, a library, a latrine and a triumphal arch.

○ **SIZE:**
2,381,741 sq km

◉ **POPULATION:**
40,264,000

○ **CURRENCY:**
Algerian dinar

● **CAPITAL:**
Algiers

○ **LANGUAGES:**
Arabic, French, Berber

Tunisia

AFRICA

* Tunisian plants include date palms and olive, citrus, cork and eucalyptus trees
* El Djem's colossal Roman era amphitheatre (built 238 c.e.) could hold 35,000 spectators

Gaze out to the Mediterranean from my north African coast, and you can see the Italian island of Sicily on a clear day. My people have worked out exactly how to farm my land: they grow vegetables in my wetter northern region, olives in my central Sahel plain and dates in my southern Sahara desert. Hot? Just burrow! In Matmata, my cool, earth-sheltered dwellings are tunnelled into artificial craters – one even served as Luke Skywalker's home on the planet Tatooine. Or do a breezy island hop: Djerba, connected to my mainland by a Roman-era causeway, is said to be the island of forgetful lotus eaters in Homer's epic poem *The Odyssey*.

Care to shop in the *souk*? Imagine jute sacks of red harissa spice, saffron and cinnamon; couscous in ancient canisters; brass lanterns; and piles of oriental carpets. But how to get around? Never mind used-car lots: I offer camel markets, where you can roam between rows of rope-bridled camels looking for a new home. Dare to take one for a spin?

○ **SIZE:**
163,610 sq km

● **POPULATION:**
11,135,000

○ **CURRENCY:**
Tunisian dinar

● **CAPITAL:**
Tunis

○ **LANGUAGE:**
Arabic

Libya
AFRICA

* Brome grass, canary grass, bluegrass and rye grass grow on Libya's coastal plains
* Tripoli's museum of history has an exhibit of former dictator Colonel Gaddafi's cars

SIZE:
1,759,540 sq km

POPULATION:
6,542,000

CURRENCY:
Libyan dinar

CAPITAL:
Tripoli

LANGUAGE:
Arabic

Once a poor land of Berber nomads who roamed the Sahara desert, I struck it rich when gas companies drilled down to my oily depths in 1959. But in recent years, civil war has reduced my oil industry to a dribble.

In the days before Christianity, I was split in two: eastern Cyrenaica, colonized by the Phoenicians, and western Tripolitania, the province of the Greeks. Both regions became outposts of the Roman Empire; my Roman ruins in Leptis Magna feature ancient archways topped with huge heads of the monster Medusa. In my north-eastern village oasis, Ghadames, age-old homes have been modelled from mud, lime and palm tree trunks. Like honeycombed caves, they give protection from the brutal desert sun. The Ubari sand sea is a vast area of sculpted dunes with 20 palm-fringed, salty micro lakes; 200,000 years ago, the area was one enormous lake. At Al-Harüj al-Aswad at my centre, remnants of ancient lava streams form a vast black, basalt plateau that rises 2800 metres out of the sand.

Egypt
AFRICA

* The tomb of the young pharaoh Tutankhamen lay undiscovered for more than 3000 years
* The hunting dog of the pharaohs is related to today's Ibizan Hound dog breed

○ **SIZE:**
1,001,450 sq km

◉ **POPULATION:**
94,667,000

○ **CURRENCY:**
Egyptian pound

● **CAPITAL:**
Cairo

○ **LANGUAGE:**
Arabic

Can I just say? I'm more than my ancient past! I'm like a rock star forced to replay the old hits. Spin the Sphinx again, baby! Man, play those Pyramids one more time.

I'm high tech, alright? I connected the Mediterranean and Red Seas by building the Suez Canal (in 1869) *and* I harnessed the Nile River by building the Aswan High Dam (opened 1970). To build the dam, which provides a renewable source of energy for electricity, my guys had to dig out 44 million cubic metres of rubble and earth. They also had to dismantle my colossal Abu Simbel temple complex, rock by rock, to rebuild it on higher ground. Oh, and the practice of irrigation started on my land, when ancient Egyptians (yes, OK, those guys again) sowed seeds in muddy land left by the annual flooding of the Nile River.

Mauritania

AFRICA

Almost entirely desert, I'm the ancient route for trans-Saharan camel caravans, packing sacks of gold and dates to trade in my coastal capital. On the way, they'd have passed an oasis or two and the Guelb er Richat – a curious rock structure that looks like a bull's-eye from outer space. My old Islamic pilgrimage city, Chinguetti, is the site of the 13th-century Friday Mosque, with its simple, square stone minaret and treasure of medieval Islamic manuscripts.

- **SIZE:** 1,030,700 sq km
- **POPULATION:** 3,677,000
- **CURRENCY:** Mauritanian ouguiya
- **CAPITAL:** Nouakchott
- **LANGUAGE:** Arabic

Senegal

AFRICA

I'm a country of rolling, sandy plains whose capital serves three key shipping lanes. The heron-friendly Senegal River forms a natural border to my north, and forest and mangrove swamps fringe my southern edge. Although my people are 90 per cent Muslim, the influences of former French colonizers and Arabic North Africa have infused their culture. You'll see printed cotton fabrics styled into classic head wraps and flowing caftan-like robes.

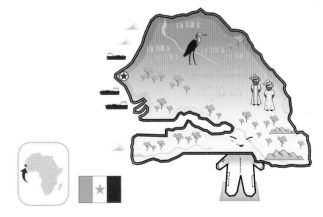

- **SIZE:** 196,722 sq km
- **POPULATION:** 14,320,000
- **CURRENCY:** CFA franc
- **CAPITAL:** Dakar
- **LANGUAGES:** French, Wolof

The Gambia

AFRICA

* Arab traders brought Islam to this country; today's population is 90 per cent Muslim
* Apart from its short coastline, The Gambia is entirely surrounded by Senegal

○ **SIZE:**
11,300 sq km

◉ **POPULATION:**
2,010,000

○ **CURRENCY:**
Gambian dalasi

◉ **CAPITAL:**
Banjul

○ **LANGUAGES:**
English, Mandinka

I resemble a wiggly finger rudely tickling Senegal's tummy. My territory borders both sides of the Gambia River as it meanders toward the Atlantic.

My poor soil quality means that most farming on my land is subsistence-level – people grow just enough food to eat. Peanuts are a major crop and feature in *domoda*, a stew made with peanut butter, tomato, chilli pepper, pumpkin and lemon. My namesake river is both a blessing and a curse. Navigable along its length, the river ends at Banjul, a bustling port on the Atlantic coast. In the 1700s, thousands of Africans were transported to the Americas from here, to work as slaves. If you take a twilight stroll along the river, look for Gambian epauletted fruit bats heading out to hang in the nearest mango grove. Their "epaulettes" are little tufts of hair on their shoulders.

Guinea-Bissau

AFRICA

A mostly low-lying, tropical, swamp-like place, my land rises to grassland and forest in the east. To the west, my Bijagós archipelago features 88 offshore tropical islands – home to dolphins and manatees. I also attract 96 species of migratory birds. Big fishing fleets are scared off by the sand bars between my islands, so the solitary angler rules here. Cashew! No, I didn't sneeze, I'm just bragging about my major nutty export.

- **SIZE:** 36,125 sq km
- **POPULATION:** 1,760,000
- **CURRENCY:** CFA franc
- **CAPITAL:** Bissau
- **LANGUAGES:** Portuguese, Guineau-Bissau Creole

Guinea

AFRICA

A republic on the western coast of Africa, I have a patchwork terrain of coastal mangrove swamps yielding to flat grassy plains and both lowland and mountain forests alternating with savannah. My capital, on Tombo island, is linked to the Kaloum peninsula mainland by a causeway. Not only am I mineral rich, being chock-full of bauxite, but I'm one of Africa's wettest countries; my Mount Nimba nature reserve has 50 springs.

- **SIZE:** 245,857 sq km
- **POPULATION:** 12,093,000
- **CURRENCY:** Guinean franc
- **CAPITAL:** Conakry
- **LANGUAGE:** French

Sierra Leone

AFRICA

My long Atlantic coastline is backed by green hills lush with coconut and banana trees. In recent years, an outbreak of the deadly Ebola virus had devastating effects, but I am getting back on track. And I have much to be proud of: my capital, Freetown, was founded by freed slaves; in 2017, the generosity of my people was shown when a part-time diamond miner found a 706-carat diamond – and donated it to my treasury.

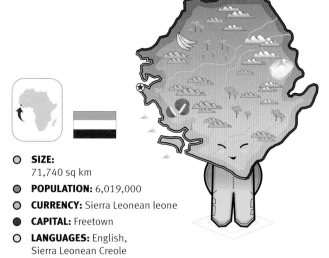

- ○ **SIZE:** 71,740 sq km
- ◉ **POPULATION:** 6,019,000
- ○ **CURRENCY:** Sierra Leonean leone
- ● **CAPITAL:** Freetown
- ○ **LANGUAGES:** English, Sierra Leonean Creole

Liberia

AFRICA

Founded in the early 19th century by freed slaves sent back from America, my name is a play on the word "liberty". From rolling plains along my coast, I'm a hilly place once you get inland, and I have a cluster of low mountains in my north-east. I'm rich in diamonds, iron ore and timber. Europeans used to call me the Pepper Coast for my spicy malagueta pepper, once my main export.

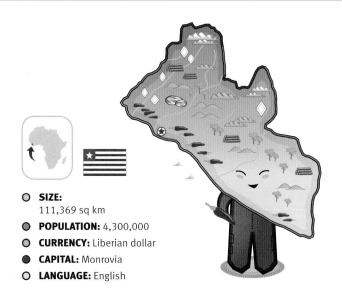

- ○ **SIZE:** 111,369 sq km
- ◉ **POPULATION:** 4,300,000
- ○ **CURRENCY:** Liberian dollar
- ● **CAPITAL:** Monrovia
- ○ **LANGUAGE:** English

Ivory Coast
AFRICA

☀ French is the official language here, but over 70 indigenous languages are spoken
☀ The Basilica of Our Lady of Peace in Yamoussoukro is the largest church in the world

Prince of pods – the world's premier producer of cocoa – I am a chocolate-maker's dream. I owe my status as West Africa's most profitable economy to cocoa beans, although I also produce coffee, rubber, sustainable palm oil, mahogany – and in the past, ivory from elephant tusks. I was once known as the Côte des Dents – "Coast of Teeth" – for my ivory chops!

Growing crops for export encourages deforestation – chopping down forests to make room for mono-cropping. It is a profitable business, so squatters steal and destroy my forest to grow cocoa illegally. And when forests disappear, so do my pygmy hippos, elephants and pangolins, as well as colobus monkeys and many other primates. My people are creative, though. Korhogo cloth, made by the Senufo tribe, is handmade cotton painted with traditional symbols using fermented mud paint. And the beautiful wooden sculptures and masks of the Baule artisans influenced modern European artists such as Picasso and Modigliani.

○ **SIZE:**
322,463 sq km

◑ **POPULATION:**
23,740,000

○ **CURRENCY:**
CFA franc

● **CAPITAL:**
Yamoussoukro

○ **LANGUAGE:**
French

Ghana

AFRICA

* Lake Volta, the world's largest artificial lake, provides hydroelectric power
* The poisonous cobra and puff adder snakes are native to Ghana

You could say I had the golden touch – my land was once the centre of the famous Ashanti Empire, a West African tribal power at its height from the 17th to 19th centuries. Founder King Osei Tutu conquered other tribes and produced the Golden Stool, a kind of throne that he claimed had floated out of the sky and landed in his lap – a sign that he was the divinely anointed ruler! I was once known as the Gold Coast, and the Ashantis prospered by trading in gold and selling slaves. Their descendants are still my largest tribe.

Butterflies. More than 650 species of the winged beauties flutter over my land – twice the number found in Europe. Baobabs. My people love those trees of mine, eating their gourd-like fruit and making barrels from their trunks. They even fashion clothing from the bark. And baskets. Kente cloth is a traditional textile art of my Ashanti and Ewe tribes. The name Kente means "basket", referring to the interweaving of vibrantly coloured, geometric-patterned strips.

○ **SIZE:**
239,000 sq km

● **POPULATION:**
26,908,262

○ **CURRENCY:**
Ghanaian cedi

● **CAPITAL:**
Accra

○ **LANGUAGE:**
English

Togo

AFRICA

A thin slip of a country, I'm mostly marshy mangroves to my south and tropical savannah to my north – expect to see an elephant or a leopard. My Mono River runs down at least two-thirds of my length. I'm a bit murky (in Ewe language, my name means "land where lagoons lie"), but primitive? Hardly. Sophisticated scholars of earth-friendly architecture scurry here to study my *takienta*, the mud tower houses of my Batammariba people.

- ○ **SIZE:** 56,785 sq km
- ● **POPULATION:** 7,757,000
- ○ **CURRENCY:** CFA franc
- ● **CAPITAL:** Lomé
- ○ **LANGUAGE:** French

Benin

AFRICA

L ike Togo, I'm narrow with a short, mangrove coastline. The Mono River acts as a boundary between us to the south and we share the Atakora mountain range to my north-east. In my city of Ouidah, my Temple of the Sacred Python – full of free-wriggling reptiles – commemorates a legend that describes forest pythons protecting my ancient King Kpassé during a war. French cabaret meets Congolese rumba in the folk music of my people.

- ○ **SIZE:** 112,622 sq km
- ● **POPULATION:** 10,741,000
- ○ **CURRENCY:** CFA franc
- ● **CAPITAL:** Porto-Novo
- ○ **LANGUAGE:** French

Burkina Faso

AFRICA

- Burkina Faso's Nazinga Reserve has the largest elephant population in West Africa
- Bwa masqueraders in black-and-white masks dance at harvest and funeral ceremonies

SIZE:
274,200 sq km

POPULATION:
19,513,000

CURRENCY:
CFA franc

CAPITAL:
Ouagadougou

LANGUAGE:
French

A landlocked former French colony, my climate is arid and hot, my soil is poor and I'm subject to that most ancient of plagues: the desert locust. Still, I usually take the annual prize as Africa's most productive producer of cotton!

My village of Tiébélé, home to the royal court of the Kassena ethnic group since the 15th century, is famed for its earthen homes built from a mush of mud, straw, cow dung and chalk. Strengthened with a "secret-sauce" varnish made from locust beans, the structures are elaborately painted with vibrant symbolic designs. The villagescape includes mausoleums, as the dead are laid to rest inside the village walls. Elsewhere, my people work to the bouncing beat of *balafons*, or get down to *djembes* – just a few of my traditionally crafted drums.

* To the north of Mali lies the Sahara desert; to the south is tropical savannah
* A large sandstone mound, La Main de Fatima, resembles an upraised hand

My story focuses on sun, sand and salt. In the old days of the Mali Empire (13th–16th centuries), nomadic Tuareg traders in salt, gold, silk and slaves clambered onto camels to travel in caravans between my fabled trading post Timbuktu, on the Niger River, and Mediterranean ports. The Tuaregs were known as the "blue people" because they used my native *Indigofera* plant to dye their robes and turbans. (It also dyed their skin blue!)

My Dogon people have inhabited the Bandiagara escarpment since Paleolithic times. Set into the rocks, their cave-like dwellings have neither electricity nor plumbing! These spiritual people are known for their incredible rock art and for a ritualistic funeral dance that features masks towering 60 centimetres high. Interaction with people from the Middle East brought the Islamic faith. Today, Djenné, an ancient centre of Islamic learning, is home to the Great Mosque, the world's largest mud-brick building.

○ **SIZE:**
1,240,192 sq km

◐ **POPULATION:**
17,467,000

○ **CURRENCY:**
CFA franc

● **CAPITAL:**
Bamako

○ **LANGUAGES:**
French, Bambara

105

Niger

AFRICA

- Remains of a 110-million-year-old "Super Croc" fossil were found in the Ténéré desert
- Roasted locusts and camel milk yogurt feature in Niger's desert cuisine

SIZE:
1,267,000 sq km

POPULATION:
18,639,000

CURRENCY:
CFA franc

CAPITAL:
Niamey

LANGUAGE:
French

Known for desert, drought and deadly wildlife, I'm home to the deathstalker scorpion and the horned sand viper – both venomous. But did you know I also have my very own sand cat? It's an adorable domestic-looking kitty, with thick hair covering its footpads to protect them from the hot sand.

My Air and Ténéré Reserves, two linked desert regions, offer extraordinary evidence of a greener prehistoric past. In the Air Mountains, highly detailed, 5.5-metre-tall petroglyphs of giraffes suggest that, 6000 years ago, enough foliage grew here for these herbivores to prosper. In my Ténéré desert, today a stark land of sand, numerous human skeletons have been found in an ancient burial ground. Pollen evidence suggests that some of the bodies were laid to rest on beds of flowers.

Nigeria
AFRICA

- Nigeria is known for the "afrobeat" music of Fela Kuti, a songwriter and political activist
- Native Cross River gorillas and Nigeria–Cameroon chimpanzees are endangered species

Lights, camera, action! I'm made for the spotlights – life in the slow lane is not my style. I'm Africa's most populous country – Lagos, my largest city, is home to 21 million people. They all need to be kept amused, and I deliver: Nollywood, my film industry, makes more films per year than Hollywood.

My people have stratospheric style – you only need to look at the gravity-defying head wraps (*geles*) beloved of Nigerian women to see that. Even my oil – I'm the world's sixth-largest producer of petroleum – is a star: Known as "light sweet crude", it needs very little refining. America is one of my biggest customers: I'm running their wheels and warming their butts, you know!

My Niger River – Africa's third longest – forms a web of tributaries known as the Niger Delta before it flows into the Gulf of Guinea. The delta's mangrove swamps and rainforests are where my wildlife hang out – monkeys, crocodiles, snakes, turtles and fish.

- **SIZE:**
  923,768 sq km
- **POPULATION:**
  186,053,000
- **CURRENCY:**
  Nigerian naira
- **CAPITAL:**
  Abuja
- **LANGUAGE:**
  English

Chad

AFRICA

- ☀ Elaborately engraved calabashes (gourds) are a traditional Chadian art
- ☀ Chad has more than 200 ethnic groups speaking over 100 languages

Landlocked, I have a northern Sahara desert region and a central belt of Sahel savannah that depend on a rainy season that is a lot less reliable than it used to be!

My Sahara desert is home to the Ounianga Lakes and the Ennedi Massif, two landscapes of startling beauty. The Ennedi's eroded sandstone rock formations look like they were imported from the planet Mars. Then there are the freshwater lakes – 18 lake oases in the middle of the Sahara, fed by underground springs. If only my Lake Chad were so lucky. Once the world's sixth-largest lake, poor Lake Chad has shrunk by over 90 per cent from its 1963 level. I blame climate change and the demands of my growing population for water to irrigate crops. Elsewhere, I have valuable resources – oil and, in my northern Tibesti mountains (extinct volcanoes, the highest elevations in the Sahara), geothermal springs, minerals and metals such as uranium, tungsten and natron (the salt that the ancient Egyptians used to dry mummies).

- ○ **SIZE:**
  1,284,000 sq km
- ◑ **POPULATION:**
  11,852,000
- ○ **CURRENCY:**
  CFA franc
- ● **CAPITAL:**
  N'Djamena
- ○ **LANGUAGES:**
  Arabic, French

Cameroon

AFRICA

Coast, savannah, desert, rainforest, mountains – it's all here, plus at least 250 ethnic tribes who speak over 270 languages. My traditional homes include cooling Musgum mud huts inscribed with beautifully detailed patterns and, in the rainforest, bark huts with conical thatched roofs. My drill monkeys – so shy – are hard to miss as they flee deep into the rainforest, their retreating backsides flashing mauve, pink and blue.

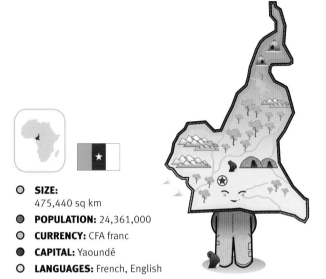

- ○ **SIZE:** 475,440 sq km
- ● **POPULATION:** 24,361,000
- ○ **CURRENCY:** CFA franc
- ● **CAPITAL:** Yaoundé
- ○ **LANGUAGES:** French, English

Equatorial Guinea

AFRICA

My landscape features coastal volcanic islands and the Rio Muni rainforest. My most populous ethnic group is the Bantu-speaking Fang; fierce jungle fighters, famed for a call-and-response-style music played on the *tam tam*, an animal-skin drum and the *mvet*, a bamboo harp. The black volcanic sand of my Ureca beaches attracts sea turtles, come egg-laying time. Even in my capital nature rules: check out the 70-metre-high silk cotton trees.

- ○ **SIZE:** 28,051 sq km
- ● **POPULATION:** 759,000
- ○ **CURRENCY:** CFA franc
- ● **CAPITAL:** Malabo
- ○ **LANGUAGES:** Spanish, French

Central African Republic

AFRICA

Landlocked, I lie at Africa's geographic centre. Well-watered by the Ubangi and Sangha rivers, my northern savannah gives way to dense tropical rainforest in the south. My hunter-gatherer people, the BaAka, retain the impressive survival talents of early humans, skilled at hunting with nets, poison-tipped arrows and crossbows. And they have a rich variety of wildlife to stalk: monkeys, antelopes and crocodiles for starters.

○ **SIZE:** 622,984 sq km

◉ **POPULATION:** 5,507,000

○ **CURRENCY:** CFA franc

● **CAPITAL:** Bangui

○ **LANGUAGES:** French, Sango

Congo

AFRICA

Slashed in two by the Equator and bordered by the Congo River, mine is a sparsely populated land with a short coastline to the south-west. Clever chimps in my Goualougo Triangle rainforest show that they are masters at using tools, such as slender, sharp sticks to penetrate termite nests. According to legend, the Mokele-Mbembe – a giant reptile – lurks in my fearsome Likouala Swamp, an area of 140,000 square kilometres.

○ **SIZE:** 342,000 sq km

◉ **POPULATION:** 4,852,000

○ **CURRENCY:** CFA franc

● **CAPITAL:** Brazzaville

○ **LANGUAGE:** French

Gabon
AFRICA

* Tribal leaders wear elaborate masks to perform traditional rituals and ceremonies
* Birdwatchers flock to Lake Oguemoué in the hope of spotting an African finfoot

Neatly cut in half by the Equator, my terrain is a happy mash-up of coastal lagoons, mountain ranges, savannah and lush rainforest. The Ogooué River cuts across my middle, spreading tentacles of tributaries through my interior reaches. My capital city, Libreville (Freetown), was founded by slaves liberated by the French Navy from a Brazilian slave ship. Africa's least densely populated country, I'm richly resourced – I've got a long Atlantic coastline with white sand beaches, oil, timber, manganese, gold and iron.

The first European sighting of a gorilla (in 1856, by the French zoologist Paul Du Chaillu) was made on my land; hardly surprising given my possession of the Earth's second-largest jungle zone. And my bugs are ablaze! Well, not exactly, but they do glow in the dark. My fire centipedes are bioluminescent – they light up when you touch them . . . but watch out, these critters' bites are full of venom!

SIZE:
267,667 sq km

POPULATION:
1,739,000

CURRENCY:
CFA franc

CAPITAL:
Libreville

LANGUAGE:
French

Democratic Republic of the Congo

AFRICA

* Kinshasa and Congo's capital Brazzaville sit opposite each other on the Congo River
* Natural resources include diamonds, cobalt, copper and petroleum

Wow! Where to start? Everywhere you look, you'll find some kind of natural marvel. Take the mighty Congo River – Africa's second largest – which winds its way across the continent, its amazing journey ending at my Matadi port. Or maybe I can tempt you to visit one of my nine enormous nature reserves to see giraffes, okapis, hippos, rhinos and forest elephants roaming wild. Up high, you'll see the peak of my glowing stratovolcano, Mount Nyiragongo, a steaming lava lake filling its centre. Down below, you'll find mines dug for cobalt minerals – your i-Phone won't charge without them. Rumour has it my streams are laced with diamonds; for sure, mountain gorillas inhabit my lush rainforests.

Sounds idyllic, I know, but life here is hard. Only nine per cent of my 65 million people have electricity at home. The animals in my nature reserves are in danger from poachers. And sometimes children get sent to work in the cobalt mines instead of going to school.

○ **SIZE:**
2,344,858 sq km

◉ **POPULATION:**
81,331,000

○ **CURRENCY:**
Congolese franc

● **CAPITAL:**
Kinshasa

○ **LANGUAGE:**
French

Sudan

AFRICA

Before 2011 and my break with South Sudan, I was Africa's largest country, an ancient Nubian civilization known as Kush, lying where the Blue and White Nile rivers meet. I boast more pyramids than Egypt in my Meroe and Nuri deserts! In Karima, my tabletop mountain, Jebel Barkal, is the legendary home of the ancient Egyptian god Amun. But don't get caught up in my desert sandstorm *haboob*, a blinding cloud of swirling dust.

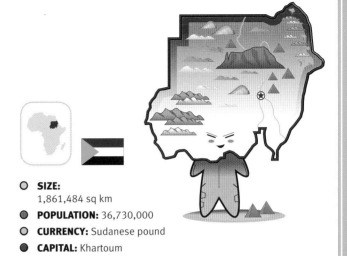

- ○ **SIZE:** 1,861,484 sq km
- ● **POPULATION:** 36,730,000
- ○ **CURRENCY:** Sudanese pound
- ● **CAPITAL:** Khartoum
- ○ **LANGUAGES:** Arabic, English

South Sudan

AFRICA

Rich with oil, I'm still underdeveloped, thanks to decades of civil war. My vast Sudd Swamp, where the White Nile spills over into my wide basin grasslands, offers a refuge for crocodiles lurking in papyrus marshes and migrating elephant herds. The Imatong Mountains on my Ugandan border serve as a water reserve for my capital. In my Boma region live the Suri people, pastoral cow herders known for their ritual *donga* (stick fights).

- ○ **SIZE:** 644,329 sq km
- ● **POPULATION:** 12,531,000
- ○ **CURRENCY:** South Sudanese pound
- ● **CAPITAL:** Juba
- ○ **LANGUAGE:** English

Eritrea

AFRICA

My capital, Asmara, showcases 1930s-era Art Deco architecture, a legacy from my time as an Italian colony. I sit on the Afar Triangle, where three of the Earth's tectonic plates meet up to rumble: active underground volcanoes spew magma that rises through my crust, hardens and sinks, lowering my land. *Teff* anyone? This staple food is one of several crops grown here; agriculture employs 80 per cent of my population.

- **SIZE:** 117,600 sq km
- **POPULATION:** 5,870,000
- **CURRENCY:** Eritrean nakfa
- **CAPITAL:** Asmara
- **LANGUAGES:** Tigrinya, Arabic, English

Djibouti

AFRICA

Craving a salty snack? Try an Afar salt pearl – spheres of salt dug from my Lac Assal, the continent's lowest elevation. My Afar people, known for their butter-sculpted dreadlocks, have for centuries led camel caravans across the lake to collect salt to trade. Ancient forests in my north give way to desert plains, while Lake Abbe, on my western border, fronts a landscape of tall limestone smokestacks belching sulfurous steam jets.

- **SIZE:** 23,200 sq km
- **POPULATION:** 847,000
- **CURRENCY:** Djiboutian franc
- **CAPITAL:** Djibouti City
- **LANGUAGES:** French, Arabic

Somalia

AFRICA

- ❋ Livestock counts toward Somalia's main exports: cattle, sheep, goats and camels
- ❋ Cows with large horns feature in ancient cave paintings at Laas Gaal (9000 B.C.E.)

Someday, I'm going to be a superstar. With my palm-tree-lined coastline – Africa's longest – it should be a cinch!

You won't get farther east than me on this continent; a peninsula on the eastern "horn" of Africa, I jut into the Indian Ocean. Apart from the Cal Madow mountain range in my north-east, my landscape remains remarkably flat and desert-like. This, combined with an extremely arid climate, makes it hard to grow food and harsh famines are not uncommon.

My people are known for their elegant features, their rich story-telling tradition, their exotic trades and a cuisine that betrays South-east Asian influences. They climb rocky cliffs to search for wild frankincense trees so they can scrape out the precious, fragrant resin. My Islamic heritage is ancient: the Fakhr-al-Din Mosque (1269) in my capital Mogadishu is built of coral blocks and features two blue minarets, side by side, one dome-shaped and one cone-shaped.

○ **SIZE:**
637,657 sq km

◉ **POPULATION:**
10,817,000

○ **CURRENCY:**
Somali shilling

◉ **CAPITAL:**
Mogadishu

○ **LANGUAGES:**
Somali, Arabic

115

Ethiopia

AFRICA

* In 1972, a 3.2-million-year-old hominid skeleton, "Lucy", was unearthed in the Rift Valley
* The Ethiopian wolf is the world's most endangered member of the dog family

SIZE:
1,104,300 sq km

POPULATION:
102,374,000

CURRENCY:
Ethiopian birr

CAPITAL:
Addis Ababa

LANGUAGES: Oromo, Amharic

The earliest known fossils of *Homo sapiens* were found right here – that fills me with pride. The Rift Valley slices through my highly elevated central plateau, sometimes called the roof of Africa; seven alkaline lakes pool within the canyon formed by the rift. My Danakil Depression, the lowest, hottest place in Africa, is formed by two separating tectonic plates. It'll cool off someday when the split gets so wide that the Red Sea spills in!

My famous eleven Lalibela churches were cut (in the 12th century) out of volcanic rock. Visit the church at Aksum, the ruins of an ancient trading city on my northern border. According to legend, the church harbours the ark of the covenant – a chest that holds the original stone tablet with the ten commandments of the Jewish, Islamic and Christian faiths: monks guard the ark and are said not to leave their post until their death.

Kenya

* Among Kenya's biggest exports are tea, flowers and coffee
* Kenya is well known for its middle- and long-distance runners

SIZE:
580,367 sq km

POPULATION:
46,790,000

CURRENCY:
Kenyan shilling

CAPITAL:
Nairobi

LANGUAGES:
English, Kiswahili

What did I do to deserve me? When it comes to stand-out features, I rule! Ports? My port city Mombasa, basking on a coral island in the Indian Ocean, is so desirable that in Kiswahili it was known as "Island of War". The Portuguese, Arabs, Omanis and Zimba tribe have all battled for it. Mountains? Mount Kenya – an extinct volcano – splattered with remnant glaciers is the legendary throne of Ngai, high god of my Kikuyu tribe. And I guarantee my Rift Valley, formed around 20 million years ago, offers an otherworldly landscape visible from the International Space Station!

My Maasai Mara is stuffed with prey: zebras, impalas and gazillions of gazelles – heaven for prowling big cat predators. Nairobi, my very 21st-century capital city (otherwise known as the Silicon Savannah), is big on mobile-phone technology, which is great for nomads. And just south of Nairobi, I'm developing Konza Tech City, soon to be my national high-tech hub.

Uganda

AFRICA

* Lake Victoria is the world's second-largest freshwater lake
* Black-and-white colobus monkeys inhabit Entebbe's botanical gardens

I'm for the birds – they keep my spirits aloft. And with my stable, warm, wet equatorial climate and lush forests, birds just love me. I'm home to over 1000 avian species, including the great blue turaco (a dude sporting a serious midnight-blue flattop) and my national bird: the East African crowned crane, whose courtship dance moves feature fancy feats of flapping, twirling and foot stomping. My Bwindi Impenetrable Forest is home to 160 species of vine-hung trees and half the world's mountain gorilla population.

I have more lakes than any other African country. They include Lake Victoria, which I share with Tanzania and Kenya. To the west, along my Congo River border, lower slopes of my misty, snow-capped Rwenzori Mountains are cushioned by moorland and festooned with ferns, lichens and giant lobelia flowers. In my south-western foothills, semi-nomadic cattle herders treasure their native Ankole cattle – an ancient breed whose curved horns can measure 2.4 metres from tip to tip.

○ **SIZE:**
241,038 sq km

◑ **POPULATION:**
38,319,000

◉ **CURRENCY:**
Ugandan shilling

● **CAPITAL:**
Kampala

○ **LANGUAGE:**
English

Rwanda

AFRICA

Allow me to introduce myself as one of Africa's most pleasant and prosperous countries – a land of green hills, mountains, forests and savannahs – plus a place in which plastic bags are banned! Everything grows well here: tea, coffee, sweet potatoes, bananas and cassava. Among my residents are primates – silverback gorillas, golden monkeys – and you'll find human primates, too: the Tutsi, Hutu and Twa peoples.

○ **SIZE:**
26,338 sq km

◉ **POPULATION:** 12,988,000

○ **CURRENCY:** Rwandan franc

◉ **CAPITAL:** Kigali

○ **LANGUAGES:** Kinyarwanda, French, English

Burundi

AFRICA

So I'm small, but I also have one jaw-dropping claim to fame: The great Nile River starts here. Yep, in a little hidden spring on my Mount Kikizi. Impressed? You will be when you see my gorgeous triple-cascade Kagera Falls. And don't miss out on my mystical drumming tradition! My Royal Drummers perform at royal funerals and feasts. Their drums are stored like precious jewels in sanctuaries located in sacred groves.

○ **SIZE:**
27,830 sq km

◉ **POPULATION:** 11,099,000

○ **CURRENCY:** Burundian franc

◉ **CAPITAL:** Bujumbura

○ **LANGUAGES:** Kirundi, French, English

Tanzania

AFRICA

* Tanzania's Serengeti National Park is home to huge herds of gazelles and zebras
* A Maasai tribesman discovered blue tanzanite in Mount Kilimanjaro's foothills

Two countries merged to form me in 1964, leaving me the legacy of their names, Tanganyika and Zanzibar. Exotic names rule: Dar es Salaam, my Indian Ocean port city, means "abode of peace" in Arabic.

Around three million years ago, one of my volcanoes collapsed inward to form my Ngorongoro Crater, a region now home to Africa's densest concentration of "big five" game: lion, leopard, elephant, Cape buffalo and rhino. Just west of the collapsed crater in Laetoli, an 23-metre trail of three-million-year-old ashy footprints helped archaeologists decide just when humans began to walk upright on two feet.

African violets and impatiens, two of the world's most common house and yard plants, are native to my shady, humid Usambara Mountains. Mount Kilimanjaro, the world's highest free-standing mountain, is really a million-year-old heap of hardened volcanic ash, lava, pumice and tephra (rock fragments).

○ **SIZE:**
947,300 sq km

◑ **POPULATION:**
52,483,000

○ **CURRENCY:**
Tanzanian shilling

● **CAPITAL:**
Dodoma

○ **LANGUAGES:**
English, Swahili

Malawi

AFRICA

I'm known as the "warm heart of Africa" and for the sunrises and sunsets reflected over my deep Lake Malawi. It also goes by the name, Calendar Lake, because it's *365* miles (587 kilometres) long, *52* miles (84 kilometres) wide and fed by *12* rivers. Its waters teem with a kaleidoscopic collection of neon-coloured fish. Time for tea? While the rest of Africa is hooked on coffee plantations, I prefer tea: I was the first African country to grow it commercially.

- ○ **SIZE:** 118,484 sq km
- ◉ **POPULATION:** 18,570,000
- ○ **CURRENCY:** Malawian kwacha
- ◉ **CAPITAL:** Lilongwe
- ○ **LANGUAGE:** English, Chichewa

Angola

AFRICA

I have oil and diamonds to boost my economy and a topography that varies wildly from flat coastal plain to steeply rising tablelands and cliffs. My interior is dominated by a high-elevation plateau. Even daredevil drivers quake at the thought of my Serra Da Leba Pass road, a series of 12 serpentine swerves with no guard rails! My national bird, the red-crested turaco, provides a splash of colour, with its green feathers, blue tail and bright-red crest.

- ○ **SIZE:** 1,246,700 sq km
- ◉ **POPULATION:** 20,172,000
- ○ **CURRENCY:** Angolan kwanza
- ◉ **CAPITAL:** Luanda
- ○ **LANGUAGE:** Portuguese

Mozambique

AFRICA

* Maputo's colonial buildings include a mint-green rail station with a wrought-iron dome
* The Zambezi River, with its Cahora Bassa dam, provides irrigation for tea and sugar crops

Tourists, come spread your beach towels on my white sands! My civil war ended in 1992 and my Portuguese colonizers finally moved on. So now I am cultivating a beachy paradise vibe. Coral reefs and island archipelagos fringe my tropical, 2500-kilometre coastline. In the Mozambique Channel off my coast, you can surf, snorkel, sail (*dhows*, slim-hulled Arab boats, are traditional) or reel in marlin, kingfish and sailfish.

My terrain consists mostly of flat coastal plains – easy on the flip-flops – that is, until you penetrate my interior. The 42,000-square-kilometre Lake Niassa reserve on my north central border is part of the East African plateau. It features miombo (a type of tree) woodland and wetlands. Lethal black mamba snakes lurk in the rocky, eroded hillocks that rise abruptly from the plain, while lions, leopards, elephants, wildebeests and zebras roam the forests. A large population of African wild dogs keeps poachers at bay.

SIZE:
799,380 sq km

POPULATION:
25,930,000

CURRENCY:
Mozambique metical

CAPITAL:
Maputo

LANGUAGE:
Portuguese

Namibia
AFRICA

* The San speak a click language that uses clicking sounds for about five consonants
* Namibia's diamond mines supply almost 30 per cent of the world diamonds

Awesome? I think I am. The word means imposing, stirring, stunning and all of these apply to my Namib and Kalahari desert landscapes, and to the hunter-gatherer culture of my San people.

I'm a land of deserts. In my coastal Namib desert (the world's oldest), the Sossusvlei sand dunes (the world's tallest) constantly change shape due to winds. Iron oxide in the sand makes them red. It's a foggy place: the Atlantic's Benguela current interacts with the ocean to send mist inland. Everything living in my severe scapes adapts for water scarcity: the bandit-masked, spear-horned oryx (a type of antelope) sucks water from succulent desert plants. The *Welwitschia mirabilis* plant grows only two long strappy leaves above ground, but a very long, deep tap root. In the inland Kalahari desert on my Botswanan border stands the quiver tree, a species of aloe. It is so-named because my hunter-gatherer San people hollow its branches to make quivers for their poison-tipped arrows.

○ **SIZE:**
824,292 sq km

◉ **POPULATION:**
2,436,000

○ **CURRENCY:**
Namibian dollar

◉ **CAPITAL:**
Windhoek

○ **LANGUAGE:**
English

Zambia

AFRICA

* Giant termite mounds of rich red soil pepper Zambia's plateau areas
* The small, native Zambian barbet snaps its bill to make a loud clicking sound

A butterfly-shaped beauty at the heart of the continent, I take my name from the Zambezi River that crosses my south-west corner. Allow me to brag (eight million straw-coloured fruit bats agree): my winey waterberries and sweet mangoes are fabulous. During their annual November migration, the bats feast in my Kasanka National Park. They form the largest gathering of fruit bats in the world, spreading the seeds of these rainforest species in their purple poo.

That whooshing noise you hear is not beating batwings, but Victoria Falls. A spectacular waterfall known locally as "the smoke that thunders", it forms part of my border with Zimbabwe. Torrents of foamy H_2O hurtle some 110 metres down into my Zambezi River gorge every second. During the dry season, the water diminishes just enough to allow risk-takers to bathe in Devil's Pool at the fall's edge – there's just a natural rock lip between the pool party-goers and the long drop.

○ **SIZE:**
752,618 sq km

◑ **POPULATION:**
15,511,000

○ **CURRENCY:**
Zambian kwacha

● **CAPITAL:**
Lusaka

○ **LANGUAGES:**
English, Bembe

Zimbabwe

AFRICA

* Prehistoric paintings of elephants and giraffes grace cave walls in the Matobo Hills
* Tobacco and gold are among Zimbabwe's biggest exports

○ **SIZE:**
390,757 sq km

◉ **POPULATION:**
14,547,000

○ **CURRENCY:**
US dollar

● **CAPITAL:**
Harare

○ **LANGUAGES:**
Shona, Ndebele, English

My name translates as "big houses of stone", after the fortifications of what was once Great Zimbabwe – the centre of my ancient Shona civilization. The walls of its 11th-century fortress were crowned with sculptures of my emblem, the bateleur eagle.

Once known as Southern Rhodesia, my journey out of the clutches of colonization has been hard fought, but like my capital, known for its vivid red flame trees and purple jacarandas, I still blossom with life and colour. The grassy *vleis* and wetlands of my Mana Pools and Hwange reserves shelter healthy populations of nearly every type of African wildlife. My Matobo Hill country is known for its wind-smoothed rock formations. And lurking in the musically named Limpopo River on my South African border, cranky crocodiles bide their time, waiting for prey.

Botswana

AFRICA

- A 1109-carat diamond discovered in 2015 is called *Lesedi La Rona* ("our light")
- Botswana's national dish is *seswaa*, a stew of meat, maize meal and greens

Rocks to riches! Diamonds are my business, and they've been good to me. Thanks to my responsible management of diamond profits, the percentage of my people in poverty has declined from 50 per cent to 19 per cent. Fills me with pride!

Meanwhile, back in my Okavango Delta, my people pole their *mokoro* canoes (hollowed from tree trunks) through the shallow waters and observe the wildlife scene. It's a cast of thousands: the striped, termite-eating aardwolves, hippos, lions, giraffes, meerkats, Cape buffalo, gnus and cheetahs. My Chobe National Park is famed for its bird species including the malachite kingfisher, known for its incredible head-first dives.

And diamonds aren't my only white mineral: my Makgadikgadi salt pan, an area the size of Switzerland, is known for its thousands of flamingos during flood season and for Chapman's baobab, a tree so large that explorers used it as a navigation beacon.

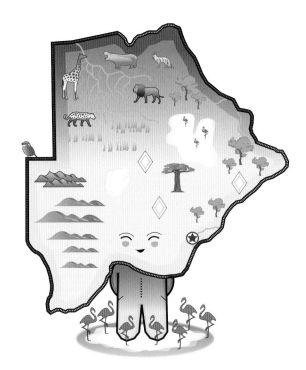

- **SIZE:**
  581,730 sq km
- **POPULATION:**
  2,209,000
- **CURRENCY:**
  Botswana pula
- **CAPITAL:**
  Gaborone
- **LANGUAGES:**
  English, Setswana

Lesotho

AFRICA

No, you are not in Switzerland, but in Lesotho – the roof of Africa. Mostly rugged Maloti Mountains, I'm known for my cool climate and Alpine fauna! Snow is common here. Due to my chill, my traditional clothing is cosy, patterned wool blanket wraps, and my huts are made of stone blocks instead of African clay or mud. Saving the best for last . . . I have my own pony, the fearless Basotho pony, named for one of my native tribes.

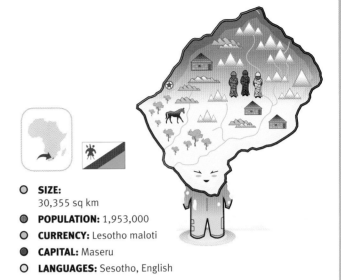

- ○ **SIZE:** 30,355 sq km
- ● **POPULATION:** 1,953,000
- ○ **CURRENCY:** Lesotho maloti
- ● **CAPITAL:** Maseru
- ○ **LANGUAGES:** Sesotho, English

Swaziland

AFRICA

Made up of forest, savannah and grassland, my territory is blessed with super-rich soil. No fewer than 2600 species of flowering plants and ferns grow here. Some, including *Kniphofia umbrina* (red-hot poker), are unique to my land. I'm big on ceremonies! For Incwala, a first-fruits celebration, men dress as warriors. Umhlanga is a reed dance – maidens dress in beaded skirts and ankle bracelets, gather reeds and dance for my royalty.

- ○ **SIZE:** 17,364 sq km
- ● **POPULATION:** 1,451,000
- ○ **CURRENCY:** Swaziland lilangeni
- ● **CAPITAL:** Mbabane
- ○ **LANGUAGES:** English, siSwati

South Africa

AFRICA

- Flat-topped Table Mountain is one of Cape Town's most recognized landmarks
- The game animals – lion, elephant, rhino, Cape buffalo, leopard – feature on bank bills
- South Africa is the world's largest producer of gold

I get shivers when I think about it: my Cape Agulhas marks the southernmost point of this great African continent. The red-and-white lighthouse on my rocky headland looks out to the meeting of the Atlantic and Indian Oceans. Most of my land sits some 1000–2100 metres up on a huge plateau, flanked to the east, south and west by a series of mountain ranges collectively known as the Great Escarpment. That big hole? That's where you'll find Lesotho – totally surrounded.

My land benefits from the winds and currents of both the Atlantic (west) and Indian (east) oceans, resulting in biodiversity that is richer than the Amazon rainforest! Eighteen thousand plant species grow in my *fynbos* region – 80 per cent of them unique! My animals range from the geometric tortoise to the Cape sugar bird. Every May, millions of sardines migrate to my shores off KwaZulu-Natal, pursued hotly by hungry sharks, seals, dolphins and humpback whales.

Besides my capital, Pretoria, important cities include coastal Cape Town (my parliament sits here) and Bloemfontein, home to my Supreme Court. I think of these cities as capitals, too. My financial centre, Johannesburg, sprouted from a gold rush.

- **SIZE:**
  1,219,090 sq km
- **POPULATION:**
  54,301,000
- **CURRENCY:**
  South African rand
- **CAPITAL:**
  Pretoria
- **LANGUAGES:**
  IsiZulu, IsiXhosa, Afrikaans, English, Sepedi, Setswana, Sesotho, Xitsonga, siSwati, Tshivenda, isiNdebele

Apartheid ("Apartness")

Racial separation played a large role in South African politics during the 20th century, affecting all areas of society. It did not end until 1994, when the country elected its first black president, Nelson Mandela.

Ancient Crater

Visible from space, the Vredefort Dome lies 100 kilometres south of Johannesburg. Created when a mountain-size piece of rock struck the Earth two billion years ago, it is not only the world's oldest crater, but also its biggest. At the time of impact it is thought to have been at least 250 kilometres wide.

Cape Verde

AFRICA

I'm an Atlantic archipelago of volcanic islands. Each one is different – from cinder heaps to lush banana and sugar-cane plantations. People even lived inside the crater of Pico, an active volcano, in huts made of volcanic rock. They grew wine in its fertile soil . . . until a 2014 eruption destroyed the village. I have a thriving dive scene: once a port of call for shipping, now my 70 undersea shipwrecks create a murky maze for scuba divers.

- **SIZE:** 4033 sq km
- **POPULATION:** 553,000
- **CURRENCY:** Cape Verdean escudo
- **CAPITAL:** Praia
- **LANGUAGES:** Portuguese, Cape Verdean Creole

São Tomé & Príncipe

AFRICA

Two tiny volcanic islands off Africa's west coast, we claim rich volcanic soil, idyllic beaches and good fishing among our riches, amid mountainous landscapes engulfed by rampant rainforest. Our indigenous creatures include the long-eared shrew and the malachite kingfisher. For dramatic flair you won't beat Auto de Floripes – a street-theatre fest with great costumes and reenactments of medieval battles between Christians and Moors.

- **SIZE:** 964 sq km
- **POPULATION:** 198,000
- **CURRENCY:** STP dobra
- **CAPITAL:** São Tomé
- **LANGUAGES:** Portuguese, Forro

Madagascar

AFRICA

* Rice, a major export, grows on terraces in the valleys of the central highlands
* The Rova, or King's Palace, stands on the capital's highest hill

Watch out! My tomato frog is so plump and red, you might accidentally put one on a pizza. Bad idea: they excrete a kind of glue. I'm a combined temperate and tropical Indian Ocean island, east of Mozambique. Around 60 million years ago, I said "au revoir" to Africa (then a super-continent known as Gondwana) and sailed off to find myself!

I evolved my very own curiosity cabinet of species, including the spear-nosed snake, the tiny Brookesia chameleon, 60 species of lemur and 1000 species of orchids. To explore, tiptoe through my Tsingy rock formations: with sharp shards of eroded limestone and karst, their name means "land where one cannot walk barefoot". Even my Malagasy people are unique: half the population have genes from Borneo, over 7240 kilometres away, suggesting that their ancestors arrived due to shipwreck! Speaking of wrecks, in 2015 a sunken ship was discovered just off my shore; the silver treasure found inside suggests it was the ship of the Scottish pirate Captain Kidd.

○ **SIZE:**
587,041 sq km

◉ **POPULATION:**
24,430,000

○ **CURRENCY:**
Malagasy ariary

◉ **CAPITAL:**
Antananarivo

○ **LANGUAGES:**
French, Malagasy

Comoros
AFRICA

Ka-boom! I'm explosive: Mount Karthala on my Grand Comore island has erupted 20 times in the past 100 years – yet the Karthala scops owl makes these volcanic slopes its home. My people aren't placid either – they've staged 20 coups since gaining independence from France. Chill, guys – try aromatherapy; it's my specialty! I'm known as "Perfume Island" for my vanilla, clove and ylang-ylang exports. Chanel No. 5 would be nothing without me!

- ○ **SIZE:** 2235 sq km
- ● **POPULATION:** 795,000
- ○ **CURRENCY:** Comorian franc
- ● **CAPITAL:** Moroni
- ○ **LANGUAGES:** Arabic, French, Shikomoro

Seychelles
AFRICA

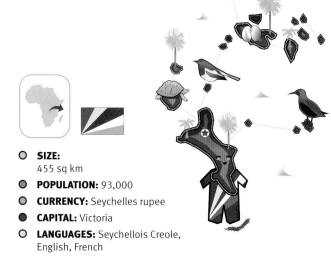

Unusual species live on my Indian Ocean archipelago of 115 granite and coral islands. Take my rare 256-legged giant millipedes – proper janitors that recycle 17 per cent of my leaf litter through their guts every 24 hours, making the soil fertile enough to support my coco de mer tree, among others. My Aride Island attracts giant Aldabra tortoises and endangered native birds: the gray sooty noddy and the blue-black magpie robin.

- ○ **SIZE:** 455 sq km
- ● **POPULATION:** 93,000
- ○ **CURRENCY:** Seychelles rupee
- ● **CAPITAL:** Victoria
- ○ **LANGUAGES:** Seychellois Creole, English, French

Mauritius

- ❊ Mauritius has depended on sugar production ever since colonial times
- ❊ In the popular folk dance, the *sega*, a dancer's feet never leave the ground

A small volcanic island in the Indian Ocean, I form part of the Mascarene Islands 800 kilometres east of Madagascar and am surrounded by coral reefs. My most famous native, the flightless dodo bird, went extinct long ago, leaving me and my mostly Hindu population (descendants of Indian servants imported by past European colonizers) to mind our own business. Among my features are white sand beaches favoured by dolphins and the idyllic Chamarel waterfall. Check out my seven coloured dunes – red, brown, violet, blue, green, yellow and purple – formed by iron and aluminium oxides in the sand. Or stroll across my natural stone bridges formed by pounding surf on the rockier side of my coastline.

When scientists analysed zircon crystals in my cliffs, they deduced that the cliffs were older than the rest of me – much older: I formed just nine million years ago, compared to the almost three-billion-year age of the cliffs. It seems I've been concealing the lost super-continent of Mauritia all these years!

○ **SIZE:**
2040 sq km

◐ **POPULATION:**
1,348,000

○ **CURRENCY:**
Mauritian rupee

● **CAPITAL:**
Port Louis

○ **LANGUAGES:**
English, Creole

Asia

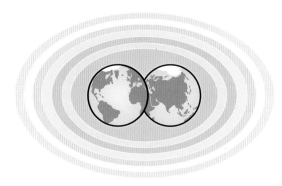

I'm sprawled out on the Earth's surface like I own it – well, I am the planet's largest, most populous continent. And although my Tibetan monks may practise the art of silence, when it comes to my history, I'm loud and proud. My Mongolian horsemen were the centaurs of the steppes; their hard riding on tough little ponies helped Genghis Khan create the Mongol Empire, history's largest continuous land empire.

* **Land mass:**
  44,579,000 sq km
* **Number of countries:** 47

I'm riding high: my Tibetan plateau, "the roof of the world", is 5 kilometres above sea level and bordered by Everest and K2, the world's two highest mountains. I'm bordered by the Ural Mountains in the west, but my south-eastern reaches harbour the most wonderful water worlds. My Badjao people are sea nomads, living on *vintas* (houseboats) and free-diving the deep to harvest pearls and fish.

* **Biggest lake:** Baikal
* **Longest river:** Yangtze
* **Highest mountain:** Everest

Asia

 Afghanistan

 Armenia

 Azerbaijan

 Bahrain

 Bangladesh

 Bhutan

 Brunei

 Cambodia

 China, People's Republic of

 East Timor

 Georgia

 India

 Indonesia

 Iran

 Iraq

 Israel

 Japan

 Jordan

 Kazakhstan

 Kuwait

 Kyrgyzstan

 Laos

 Lebanon

 Malaysia

 Maldives

 Mongolia

 Myanmar

 Nepal

 North Korea

 Oman

 Pakistan

 Philippines

 Qatar

 Saudi Arabia

 Singapore

 South Korea

 Sri Lanka

Black Sea
Georgia
Caspian Sea
Armenia
Azerbaijan
Uzbekist
Turkmenist
Turkey
Syria
Lebanon
Iraq
Iran
Mediterranean Sea
Israel
Jordan
Kuwait
Persian Gulf
Bahrain
Qatar
U.A.E.
Red Sea
Saudi Arabia
Oman
Yemen

Kazakhstan

Mongolia

Kyrgyzstan

Tajikistan

China

North
Korea

*Sea
of
Japan*

South
Korea

Japan

Afghanistan

Pakistan

*East
China
Sea*

Nepal

Bhutan

India

Bangladesh

Myanmar

Taiwan

*Pacific
Ocean*

*Arabian
Sea*

Laos

*Bay of
Bengal*

Thailand

Vietnam

Cambodia

*South
China
Sea*

*Philippine
Sea*

Philippines

Sri
Lanka

Maldives

Indian Ocean

Malaysia

Singapore

Brunei

Indonesia

*East
Timor*

Syria

Taiwan

Tajikistan

Thailand

Turkey

Turkmenistan

United Arab
Emirates

Uzbekistan

Vietnam

Yemen

Turkey

ASIA

* Ankara's tallest building, Atakule Tower, offers 360-degree views over the city
* The impressive ruins of the ancient Greek city of Ephesus stand on the coast of Ionia
* The Tigris River rises in the Taurus Mountains of eastern Turkey

My irregular shape and strategic location have been useful to my people over the centuries. You see, with three per cent of my land in south-eastern Europe (that includes my major city, Istanbul) and 97 per cent in south-western Asia, I act as a bridge between the two continents. Not only that, but my Turkish Straits, the Bosporus and Dardanelles, are the ultimate connectors between the Mediterranean and the Black Sea, between Europe, Russia and Ukraine.

Did you know I'm the site of ancient Troy, where the Greek hero Odysseus duped the Trojans by hiding an army in a massive wooden horse? Or that Mount Ararat, the enormous volcanic mountain on my border with Armenia and Iran, is the spot where Noah is said to have landed his ark?

Care to go for a spin? Check out my whirling dervishes – Islamic holy men who spin in circles to get closer to Allah. Had enough? Go to ground in Cappadocia. My central region hides over 30 underground cities and thousands of churches carved over centuries into the soft basaltic rock. Stop on the way to buy some Turkish Delight; my signature sweetmeat is dried fruits and nuts suspended in a sweet starchy gel.

- **SIZE:** 783,562 sq km
- **POPULATION:** 80,275,000
- **CURRENCY:** Turkish lira
- **CAPITAL:** Ankara
- **LANGUAGE:** Turkish

Pamukkale ("Cotton Castle")

A glistening, white landscape of terraces and waterfalls awaits visitors to Pamukkale. The forms result from the buildup of white calcite deposits carried by the local natural warm-water springs.

Holy Architecture

Two sacred buildings stand within sight of one another in Istanbul. The rosy red Hagia Sophia was built as a church in 360 c.e. and converted into a mosque in 1453. It is now a museum. Sultan Ahmed Mosque, known as the Blue Mosque for its interior blue tiles, was built in 1616.

Armenia

ASIA

I may be small, but I am also immensely old. My ancient earth is rich in minerals, notably copper (my main export) from my Kajaran mine, but also gold and even the odd diamond or two. Above ground, snap some shots of my fortresses – say, at Amberd or Bjni – before making your way to my high-altitude Lake Sevan. During my long, hot summers, locals love to hang out on the lake's beaches, eating crawfish caught in its cool waters.

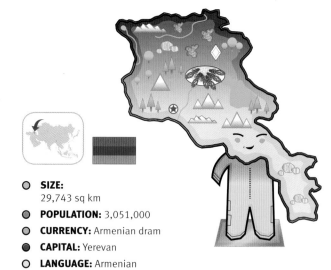

- ○ **SIZE:** 29,743 sq km
- ● **POPULATION:** 3,051,000
- ○ **CURRENCY:** Armenian dram
- ● **CAPITAL:** Yerevan
- ○ **LANGUAGE:** Armenian

Georgia

ASIA

Say "cheese" ("*qveli*") when you see me, for food is never a problem. Lush with green valleys, my highland terrain stretches east from the Black Sea. *Rtveli*, my September harvest, yields tea, peanuts and grapes galore. Scenic mountains and ancient architecture ensure superb snapshots, and wildlife is great. Be sure to catch one of my colourful native birds: a pink-breasted great rosefinch or the striking Güldenstädt's redstart.

- ○ **SIZE:** 69,700 sq km
- ● **POPULATION:** 4,928,000
- ● **CURRENCY:** Georgian lari
- ● **CAPITAL:** Tbilisi
- ○ **LANGUAGE:** Georgian

Azerbaijan
ASIA

* Azerbaijan's national animal, the Karabakh horse, is one of the world's oldest breeds
* Baku's seafront carpet museum is shaped like a rolled-up rug

○ **SIZE:**
82,629 sq km

◉ **POPULATION:**
9,873,000

○ **CURRENCY:**
Azerbaijani manat

● **CAPITAL:**
Baku

○ **LANGUAGE:**
Azerbaijani

I'm burning red-hot right now! Freedom from Soviet control (gained in 1991) has fanned my flames of ambition. My oil and gas resources have been famous since medieval times, and today, oil money is fuelling some pyrotechnic architecture – just look at my capital Baku's Flame Towers, if you don't believe me. My Baku Ateshgah is a Zoroastrian temple and monastic complex built over a natural gas well; the temple flame is fuelled by gas seeps. At Yanar Dag, on my Absheron Peninsula, gas seeping from beneath the bedrock burns permanently in an ever-burning brush fire.

My natural resources love to show off: the strawberry and white swirls of my Candy Cane Mountains (think Christmas ribbon candy) are the result of a chemical reaction between the minerals in the rocks and groundwater.

Syria

ASIA

☀ The Umayyad Mosque in the walled city of Damascus is one of the world's oldest

☀ Sand-bearing wind blows a wall of dust across the land once or twice a year

Known in ancient days as Sham, I was once famed for my swordsmiths, who honed swirl-patterned Damascus steel blades able to slice through a floating silk scarf, and for the Hurrian Hymn, the world's first melody written in musical notation – a song for the lute. But in 2011, a civil war began that ravaged my land; the sounds that shatter my skies are no longer harmonious.

The Euphrates River runs through my arid landscape – mostly desert plateau rimmed by the Bishri Mountains to the north and the Anti-Lebanon range to the west. I'm short on vegetation – blame my poor soils. You'll find citrus trees in my coastal region, date palms in the Euphrates valley and hardy evergreens on my mountain slopes. Today, my country bears the scars of air and mortar strikes, but I am no stranger to conflict. My land is scattered with Crusader-era castles, such as the 10th- century Masyaf Castle, secret hideout of the Assassins, a medieval-era Ismaili sect feared for the slaying of its religious enemies!

○ **SIZE:**
185,180 sq km

● **POPULATION:**
17,185,000

○ **CURRENCY:**
Syrian pound

● **CAPITAL:**
Damascus

○ **LANGUAGE:**
Arabic

Lebanon

ASIA

You won't guess what covers 13 per cent of my land . . . cedar trees! They grow up to 40 metres tall, and King Solomon used them to build his temple in nearby Jerusalem. People come to ski in my mountains – the name of the oldest and highest resort is Cedars Ski Resort (what else?). When done with the ski runs, head to my cosmopolitan capital by the sea, where you can chill out on the beach or ogle the superyachts moored in the marina.

- ○ **SIZE:** 10,400 sq km
- ◑ **POPULATION:** 6,238,000
- ○ **CURRENCY:** Lebanese pound
- ● **CAPITAL:** Beirut
- ○ **LANGUAGE:** Arabic

Jordan

ASIA

Guides to my ancient rock-carved site of Petra tell people it's "half as old as time". And when a movie includes action on Mars, I tell people it was probably shot in the red-sand desert at Wadi Rum. If you are not a fan of summer heat, my tip is to go float in my oh-so-salty Dead Sea or to snorkel off my teeny 26-kilometre coast on the Gulf of Aqaba. But I don't recommend being baptised in my Jordan River – it's pretty polluted these days.

- ○ **SIZE:** 89,342 sq km
- ◑ **POPULATION:** 8,185,000
- ○ **CURRENCY:** Jordanian dinar
- ● **CAPITAL:** Amman
- ○ **LANGUAGE:** Arabic

Israel

ASIA

* Archaeologists have unearthed a 2500-year-old dog cemetery at Ashkelon
* The Mount Carmel mountain range to the north is Israel's largest national park

Scout my territory, and you'll encounter sites sacred to Judaism, Christianity and Islam. On Jerusalem's Temple Mount are the Dome of the Rock, the traditional site where Muhammad made his night journey to Paradise (Islam) and where Abraham led Isaac to sacrifice (Judaism); the Stone of Unction, where Jesus's body was prepared for burial (Christianity); and the Western "Wailing" Wall, Judaism's holiest site. My sparsely settled southern Negev desert is home to *makhtesh*, deep canyons ground out by erosion that display evidence of my prehistoric past in colourful rock strata. The springs there attract ibex and Arabian leopards. The Jordan River runs south from my northern hills of Galilee to form my border with Jordan.

My territory may be ancient, but as a country I'm not even 100 years old. My creation as a homeland for Jews in 1948 displaced native Palestinians. I continue to occupy Palestinian land, such as the West Bank, and this has caused decades of bitter fighting.

○ **SIZE:**
20,770 sq km

◐ **POPULATION:**
8,175,000

○ **CURRENCY:**
Israeli new shekel

● **CAPITAL:**
Tel Aviv-Yafo

○ **LANGUAGES:**
Hebrew, Arabic

Saudi Arabia
ASIA

* Saudi's nomadic Bedouins are known for sword dancing and hunting with falcons
* King Fahd's Fountain, in the city of Jeddah, is the tallest fountain in the world

Occupying most of the Arabian Peninsula, my territory includes three major deserts: the Rub' al Khali, An Nafud and ad-Dahna – the world's largest sand-only desert expanses. The Rub' al Khali, known as the "Empty Quarter", is uninhabited – but it is crossed by kilometres of oil pipelines.

No rivers cross my terrain. So? I'm a shipping powerhouse, thanks to coastlines on both the Persian Gulf and the Red Sea. And don't forget my "desert ships" – charismatic Arabian camels that can store up to 36 kilograms of fat in their humps. Plus, there's something more precious flowing beneath me: only 265 billion barrels or so of oil! I also sit on caves: my Umm er Radhuma rock bed is pocked with limestone caverns, including a deep one known as the Father of Fear! My people drink thick coffee flavoured with ginger and cardamom. Many of them also practise an austere form of Islam known as Wahhabism, which interprets the words of the Islamic text, the Koran, strictly.

○ **SIZE:**
2,149,690 sq km

● **POPULATION:**
28,160,000

○ **CURRENCY:**
Saudi riyal

● **CAPITAL:**
Riyadh

○ **LANGUAGE:**
Arabic

145

Oman

ASIA

Come and explore my desert, camping out under the stars at night. The beautiful red and brown dunes at A'Sharqiyah Sands stretch over 98,420 square kilometres. This is Bedouin territory – take a camel ride to get a feel for the nomadic life, or speed across the sand in a dune buggy. Later, cool off in the shade at my Bahla fort, or chill on the beach at Muscat. You might spot a dolphin or two, if you're lucky.

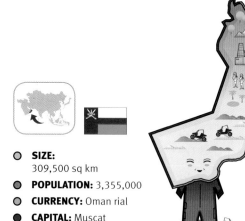

- ○ **SIZE:** 309,500 sq km
- ◑ **POPULATION:** 3,355,000
- ○ **CURRENCY:** Oman rial
- ● **CAPITAL:** Muscat
- ○ **LANGUAGE:** Arabic

Yemen

ASIA

Mud sticks – it needs to, since my most attractive feature is my mud-brick architecture: square slabs that can rise several stories high. You can see them in my capital Sana'a and at Wadi Hadhramaut skirting the edge of the Rub' al Khali desert (which I share with Saudi Arabia, Oman, and the U.A.E.). My people drink tea and coffee; my Red Sea port of Mocha was once known for exporting coffee to Europe. My honey is famous, too.

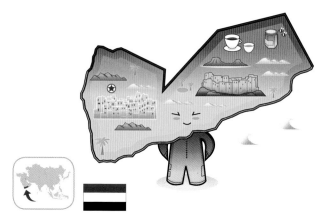

- ○ **SIZE:** 527,968 sq km
- ◑ **POPULATION:** 27,393,000
- ○ **CURRENCY:** Yemeni rial
- ● **CAPITAL:** Sana'a
- ○ **LANGUAGE:** Arabic

Iran
ASIA

* Legend says a three-headed dragon lurks at Mount Damavand, Asia's highest volcano
* The Iranians built Tehran's Azadi Tower in celebration of the Persian Empire

Don't be fooled by the plain black robes of my contemporary clerics. At heart, I revel in pattern and colour: I'm opulent, like my famed Persian carpets. Even my landscape is rich; it's rimmed by the Zagros and Alborz mountain ranges on two sides and opens to the Caspian Sea in my north and the Persian Gulf and Arabian Sea to the south, where I grow forests of wild pistachio trees. Then there is Qeshm Island off my southern coast, with its mangroves, coral reefs and Persian melons. Yes, even my food is sumptuous – pomegranates full of ruby-red seeds and my rose-water ice cream – a specialty!

My Safavid dynasty patronized artisans who created velvet and silk textiles featuring people and exotic illustrated manuscripts, such as the 15th-century *Mantiq-al-tayr* (Language of the Birds). In my Isfahan region, the birds live in castles: my people built brick and limestone dovecotes – little towers for doves tunnelled with nesting niches; the dung was collected to fertilize fields and tan my famous leather.

○ **SIZE:**
1,648,195 sq km

◑ **POPULATION:**
82,802,000

○ **CURRENCY:**
Iranian rial

● **CAPITAL:**
Tehran

○ **LANGUAGE:**
Persian

147

Iraq
ASIA

* An ancient ziggurat (a stepped stone pyramid topped by a shrine) stands in the city of Ur
* Iraq is the world's fourth-largest producer of oil

Assyria, Sumeria, Babylonia, ah, the musical names of my ancient grandeur! Gaze at the *lamassu*, stern stone guardians at the gates of my Assyrian citadels. Winged bulls with the wise heads of warrior kings symbolize the fierce pride that sustains me today, while troubled by violence and unrest.

I was once known as Mesopotamia, or the land between two rivers. The Tigris and Euphrates rivers meander in parallel down my length, then join in my southern town, Al-Qurnah; tradition says their meeting point was the location of the Garden of Eden. The plains around the rivers formed the "fertile crescent", where agriculture nourished one of the earliest civilizations. Head west from here and you'll stray into desert territory. To my south are marshlands, where my Marsh Arab people built huts of reeds and fished. Drained by order of my former ruler, Saddam Hussein, today the wetlands are being restored, attracting birds that include the sacred ibis and Mesopotamian crow.

○ **SIZE:**
438,317 sq km

◉ **POPULATION:**
38,146,000

◉ **CURRENCY:**
Iraqi dinar

● **CAPITAL:**
Baghdad

○ **LANGUAGES:**
Arabic, Kurdish

Kuwait

ASIA

Apart from my oasis at Al Jahra and a cluster of islands, my land is mostly desert. No wonder my people are seafaring folk. My marinas are full of boats, and who wouldn't want to go sailing or scuba diving in my warm waters? One of the world's smallest countries, I am blessed with oil wells that bring me wealth. I also pack a punch when it comes to architecture – just look at Al Hamra Tower in Kuwait City, or my groovy "mushroom" water towers.

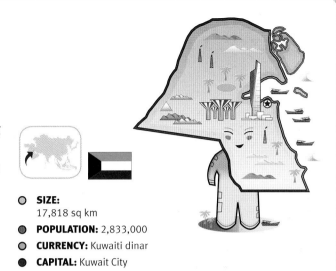

- **SIZE:** 17,818 sq km
- **POPULATION:** 2,833,000
- **CURRENCY:** Kuwaiti dinar
- **CAPITAL:** Kuwait City
- **LANGUAGE:** Arabic

Bahrain

ASIA

Even if you amount to just one small island, you can always expand! Take my Petal Beach resort and the Amwaj Islands in the shallow seas around me – all artificial! Just zip from my mainland on Avenue 59 to check out my Floating City. Many of my residents are from abroad, and plenty come for the motor racing at the Bahrain International Circuit. If cars are not your thing, take a desert safari or head to my Royal Camel Farm at Manama.

- **SIZE:** 760 sq km
- **POPULATION:** 1,379,000
- **CURRENCY:** Bahraini dinar
- **CAPITAL:** Manama
- **LANGUAGE:** Arabic

Qatar

ASIA

Trading pearls used to be my specialty, but people mostly talk about my oil these days. And why not? It has made me rich, after all. Just take a look at my skyscraper skyline in Doha – best appreciated from a Persian Gulf cruise on a traditional wooden *dhow*. Or you might just prefer to go shopping in my centuries-old Souq Waqif or visit I. M. Pei's spectacular Museum of Islamic Art on its own specially created island.

- **SIZE:** 11,586 sq km
- **POPULATION:** 2,258,000
- **CURRENCY:** Qatari riyal
- **CAPITAL:** Doha
- **LANGUAGE:** Arabic

United Arab Emirates

ASIA

Marhaba – Welcome! A federation of seven emirates that include Abu Dhabi and Dubai, my land is dotted with sculptures of the *dallah*, an Arabic coffee pot, as a mark of my hospitality. You may also spot the odd peregrine falcon – my people love falconry – or the handsome Arabian oryx, my national animal. The world's tallest structure, the Burj Khalifa, stands in Dubai, overlooking amazing (artificial) palm-shaped islands.

- **SIZE:** 83,600 sq km
- **POPULATION:** 5,927,000
- **CURRENCY:** Emirati dirham
- **CAPITAL:** Abu Dhabi
- **LANGUAGE:** Arabic

Kazakhstan

ASIA

* Astana's skyscrapers include the 150-metre-tall observation Bayterek Tower
* Ibex and mountain sheep roam Aksu-Zhabagly nature reserve

SIZE:
2,724,900 sq km

POPULATION:
18,360,000

CURRENCY:
Kazakh tenge

CAPITAL:
Astana

LANGUAGES:
Kazakh, Russian

The world's largest landlocked country, I stretch my expanse of grass, shrub land and mountains across two continents, from Europe to Asia. Horsemen once rode galloping steeds across my steppes and my people still feel at home on horseback to this day. Put it down to a history of nomadic mobility – Kazakhstan means "land of the wanderers" – and the fact that horse sausage and fermented mare's milk are delicacies here!

Would you believe that *Malus sieversii*, one of the apple's key ancestors, grows in my Altai Mountains? And that wild tulips are native to my steppes?

Modern Kazakhs live in cities such as Astana, and enjoy a booming economy created by my oil and mineral wealth. They can marvel at the Khan Shatyr, a modernistic mall that looks like a traditional Kazakh yurt (tent).

Uzbekistan

ASIA

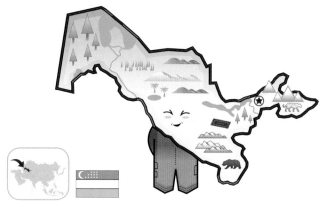

Dry and crusty, that's me! My deserts and mountains are landlocked, and my rivers never reach the sea. But, with four good seasons a year, wildlife thrives in my forests and green valleys; you might just be lucky enough to spot a snow leopard or brown bear. My ancient cities of Bukhara and Samarkand – once stopping places on the old Silk Road from China – are still known for making rugs and fine embroidery.

○ **SIZE:**
447,400 sq km

● **POPULATION:** 29,474,000   ● **CAPITAL:** Tashkent

◐ **CURRENCY:** Uzbekistani so'm   ○ **LANGUAGE:** Uzbek

Turkmenistan

ASIA

The Amu River flows through my north-east; to the south lie mountains. In between, crossed by camels, my vast deserts are so full of gas and oil that I can supply energy to my neighbours. The Silk Road once passed through my territory – you'll see the ruins of Merv, once considered the largest metropolis in the world – so it is not surprising that my national costumes, embroidered with birds and flowers, are often made of silk.

○ **SIZE:**
488,100 sq km

◐ **POPULATION:** 5,291,000   ● **CAPITAL:** Ashgabat

◐ **CURRENCY:** Turkmen manat   ○ **LANGUAGE:** Turkmen

Kyrgyzstan
ASIA

- ❋ The world's largest wild walnut forest grows in the Jalal-Abad region of Kyrgyzstan
- ❋ The agile snow leopard thrives in the rugged, sparsely populated terrain

- ○ **SIZE:**
  199,951 sq km
- ◉ **POPULATION:**
  5,728,000
- ○ **CURRENCY:**
  Kyrgyzstani som
- ● **CAPITAL:**
  Bishkek
- ○ **LANGUAGE:**
  Kyrgyz

Eighty per cent of my land is covered by the Tian Shan mountain range: longer, wider and nearly as high as the Himalayas. Home is packable here: my nomadic tribes shelter in yurts – circular felt tents fixed to a wooden lattice with braids of horse, yak or camel hair. The nomads team with fearsomely taloned golden eagles to hunt from horseback! For road food, they pack *kurut* – yak milk that is boiled, then sun-dried to make hard cakes.

Traditional fashions are cosy in winter: coats of sheepskin or wolf fur, *ak kalpaks* – peaked, embroidered white felt hats – for the guys, and *elecheks*, muslin turbans wrapped with embroidered scarves for married women.

Located near Lake Issyk-Kul, my Kumtor gold mine was once a stopover on the Silk Road caravan route. Battle-axes and a gold bar have been found at the bottom of the lake.

Tajikistan

ASIA

- Tajikistan's many mountains are home to brown bears, goats and golden eagles
- Soviet-era canals help irrigate cotton plantations and vineyards

○ **SIZE:**
144,100 sq km

◑ **POPULATION:**
8,331,000

○ **CURRENCY:**
Tajikistani somoni

● **CAPITAL:**
Dushanbe

○ **LANGUAGES:**
Tajik, Russian

Hidden deep in Muslim Asia, I'm crammed to my borders with mountains: at least 50 per cent of my land is more than 3000 metres up – I hope you have a head for heights! Lakes and rivers riddle my territory and I am sure it will surprise you to learn that I possess the world's largest non-polar glacier. If you're looking for agriculture, try Fergana Valley in my north. You'll find mostly cotton, but also fruits, grains and vegetables.

My Marco Polo sheep, named after the 13th-century explorer who first described them, weigh up to 181 kilograms and sport magnificent spiralling horns. Perched high in my Pamir Mountains, my Kuh-i-Lal mine has been in business since 7 c.e. At that time it was known for rare, golden clinohumite – red-gold nuggets, like my famously sweet apricots: impossibly juicy jewels from the ancient orchards of my Isfara region.

Afghanistan

ASIA

- ✳ Afghanistan's mosques include the 15th-century Shrine of Ali in Mazar-i-Sharif
- ✳ *Ashak* is a popular dish of leek-stuffed ravioli, topped with minced meat and yogurt

- ○ **SIZE:**
  652,230 sq km
- ◉ **POPULATION:**
  33,332,000
- ○ **CURRENCY:**
  Afghan afghani
- ● **CAPITAL:**
  Kabul
- ○ **LANGUAGES:**
  Afghan Persian (Dari),
  Pashto

No stranger to conflict, I have suffered war and political instability for decades. My territory is shaky, too – just look at my fearsome Hindu Kush mountains. Due to the underthrust of the Indian tectonic plate beneath the Eurasian plate, this is one of the most earthquake-prone zones on the Earth. Running through the mountains, the Khyber Pass connects my land with Pakistan. It's been a strategic military route for centuries.

Today I may seem a monotone moonscape of somber tan, but my past is glittered with gold. My location at a crossroads of Silk Road trade routes between China, India and the Mediterranean meant that I once bustled as a commercial hub. In Tillya Tepe, west of Mazar-i-Sharif, an excavated earthen burial mound revealed a tribal prince buried with his horse, five wives and more than 20,000 pieces of gold and precious stone jewellery.

India

ASIA

- ✳ Emperor Shah Jahan built the Taj Mahal – a marble mausoleum – in memory of his wife
- ✳ India is the world's largest producer of mangoes; Indians eat the most mangoes, too
- ✳ Blackbucks – black-blanketed antelopes with spiralled horns – roam the Thar Desert

Sparse is not my style. Consider my saris, jewellery, temples and food: I'm embroidered, brocaded, appliquéd, embellished, enamelled, encrusted, inlaid, studded and highly spiced. Yup, I'm one truly ornate country! Even my outline is diamond-shaped, crowned by the perilous peaks of the Himalayas to my north and engraved by the Ganges and Indus Rivers carving out the fertile Ganges River Valley to my south. The Sundarbans, the world's largest mangrove forest, coil their twisted tangle of roots around my Bay of Bengal border with Bangladesh; flame-striped Bengal tigers wade through their swamps.

In my city of Madurai, 33,000 carved stone sculptures of animals, gods and demons adorn my Meenakshi Amman Temple, painted in rainbow hues; green parrots trained to caw "*Meenakshi*", the name of the temple goddess, squawk at the entrance to the interior sanctuary.

I even celebrate new growth in technicolour – at Holi, a holiday that follows spring's first full moon. My whole land becomes a rampaging mass of people throwing paint and pigment in the air, until all are covered in indigo blue, rose madder red, herbal green and marigold yellow powdered dyes.

- ○ **SIZE:**
  3,287,263 sq km
- ◉ **POPULATION:**
  1,266,884,000
- ○ **CURRENCY:**
  Indian rupee
- ● **CAPITAL:**
  New Delhi

- ○ **LANGUAGES:**
  Hindi, Bengali, Telugu, Marathi, Tamil, Urdu, Gujarati, Malayalam, Kannada, Oriya, Punjabi, Assamese, Kashmiri, Sindhi, Sanskrit

River Rituals

Varanasi, an ancient city on the banks of the Ganges River, is holy to Hindus. Daily morning and evening religious rituals take place on the stepped stone embankments that reach down to the water's edge.

Kashmir Dispute

India was divided in 1947, creating Pakistan in the process. One region – Kashmir – chose to remain with India. This was the government's choice, but many people in Kashmir wanted to join Pakistan. Today, the region is split between the two countries, which continue to fight over the territory. China has made a claim, too.

Pakistan

ASIA

* ❋ The name Pakistan means "Land of the Pure"
* ❋ Lahore's Minar-e-Pakistan monument towers 70 metres above Iqbal Park

I'm a very new country, created in 1947 to be a Muslim homeland after the British left India and the country was divided. To my north loom the Karakoram Mountains, including deadly K2, the world's most dangerous mountain. The Indus River flows along my entire length from north to south and empties into the Arabian Sea near Karachi; the valley around the river was the site of a highly developed farming civilization in 2500 B.C.E., known for its carved tablets representing animals and for carnelian ornaments. Shah Jahan, the greatest of the Mughal Empire emperors, who directed the creation of the Taj Mahal in India, was born in my city Lahore in 1592.

Travelling my Karakoram Highway – the world's highest paved road – from Abbottabad to Kashgar in China can get a little dicey. (Think landslides, snow avalanches, the Khunjerab Pass at 4693 metres above sea level.) My people decorate their trucks with evil-eye motifs, turning them into mobile lucky charms.

○ **SIZE:**
796,095 sq km

◑ **POPULATION:**
201,996,000

○ **CURRENCY:**
Pakistani rupee

● **CAPITAL:**
Islamabad

○ **LANGUAGES:**
Urdu, English, Punjabi

Nepal

ASIA

My stand-out feature is the world's tallest mountain, Everest, 8848 metres above sea level; only 500 climbers reach the peak each year. Others trek the Himalayas and raft down my spectacular white waters. The streets in my old city of Kathmandu lead to ancient wooden buildings, palaces and temples, such as Boudhanath Stupa, that have survived earthquakes. In Bhaktapur stands the tallest pagoda temple in the country.

- **SIZE:** 147,181 sq km
- **POPULATION:** 29,034,000
- **CURRENCY:** Nepalese rupee
- **CAPITAL:** Kathmandu
- **LANGUAGE:** Nepali

Bhutan

ASIA

A small kingdom high in the Himalayas, I'm admired for my beautiful, remote Buddhist monasteries and fortresses (*dzong*). I ask outsiders to pay around £200 a day to visit; it covers their costs while controlling tourism. More than 60 per cent of my land is protected forest, and my subtropical plains produce my unique red rice. The takin, a goat-antelope, is my national animal, and I have black bears and red pandas, too.

- **SIZE:** 38,394 sq km
- **POPULATION:** 750,000
- **CURRENCY:** Bhutanese ngultrum
- **CAPITAL:** Thimphu
- **LANGUAGES:** Dzongkha, Sharchhopka

159

Bangladesh
ASIA

My three big rivers, the Ganges, the Brahmaputra and the Meghna, tend to flood, so my resourceful people build homes that are easy to move and farm shrimp and crab for export. My city Dhaka has become a centre of the garment trade. I also produce paper, using pulp made from bamboo that grows in my Chittagong Hills. In my cities, you'll see people using cycle rickshaws. In the countryside, look for clouded leopards.

- **SIZE:** 148,460 sq km
- **POPULATION:** 156,187,000
- **CURRENCY:** Bangladeshi taka
- **CAPITAL:** Dhaka
- **LANGUAGE:** Bengali

Sri Lanka
ASIA

Ooh, I love a cup of tea, which is fortunate because my hillsides are covered in plantations that produce Ceylon tea (Ceylon's my old name). To eat, I like fishy coconut curries. That's lucky, too, because I am surrounded by the sea and coconuts grow here in their thousands. In my forests – of mahogany, ebony and teak – elephants help by lifting trunks with their trunks! You can see hundreds of them in the wild at my Uda Walawe National Park.

- **SIZE:** 65,610 sq km
- **POPULATION:** 22,235,000
- **CURRENCY:** Sri Lankan rupee
- **CAPITAL:** Sri Jayawardenepura Kotte
- **LANGUAGES:** Sinhala, Tamil

Maldives

ASIA

I am the smallest Asian country, with dozens of atolls and islands scattered across the Indian Ocean. Getting around on a traditional *dhoni* boat is fun – except in the monsoon season. Many visitors come to dive in my sapphire-blue waters, to see the colourful coral and beautiful fish, such as the butterflyfish and angelfish. My cowrie (sea-snail) shells were once used as a currency, and you will see them as a symbol on our national bank bills.

- **SIZE:** 298 sq km
- **POPULATION:** 393,000
- **CURRENCY:** Maldivian rufiyaa
- **CAPITAL:** Malé
- **LANGUAGE:** Bahasa Malaysia

Taiwan

ASIA

I'm a techno-whizz – computers are my thing. My cities are mostly coastal: ancient Tainan lies to my west and Taipei, with its famous tower, to my north. Mountains dominate my eastern territory, peaking with mighty Yushan. Rice grows on lower slopes, all lush and green in summer. In July, the Taitung festival fills my sky with hot-air balloons of all colours. Politically, China sees me as a rebel that it wants to control, but I'd rather be independent.

- **SIZE:** 35,980 sq km
- **POPULATION:** 23,465,000
- **CURRENCY:** New Taiwan Dollar
- **CAPITAL:** Taipei
- **LANGUAGE:** Mandarin Chinese

People's Republic of China
ASIA

* Ancient wonders include the Great Wall of China and an 8000-strong Terra-Cotta Army
* A popular motif, the Chinese dragon features in traditional dances and ceremonies
* Hong Kong's skyline has more skyscrapers than any other city in the world

Foreheads to the floor: you may kowtow to me! As the imperial home of the savvy sages who invented gunpowder, the mariner's compass and printing, I think I've earned a few humble bows! I give my name to the finest porcelain, and the plant that helps us all carry on – *Camellia sinensis* (that's tea to you) – was first cultivated here. I'm mad for mulberries: White mulberries feed my silkworms, and in 105 C.E., I pressed the world's first paper from chopped mulberry bark and hemp rags.

Efforts to preserve the panda's habitat in my misty, bamboo-forested Minshan and Qinling Mountains mean the crucial watersheds that flow into my Yangtze and Yellow rivers are also saved. Other inhabitants of these remote cloud forests are protected, too – the takin ox, tree-dwelling red pandas and Chinese golden pheasants. The city of Turpan, once an oasis on my Silk Road, is rimmed by the Flaming Mountains, red sandstone peaks, the erosion of which has left them looking like flames.

Nine of my cities qualify as megacities, each with more than ten million inhabitants: you can scale skyscrapers in Guangdong and Shanghai and cross numerous bridges in Chongqing. In Beijing's Forbidden City palace complex, take your pick of no fewer than 9000 rooms.

○ **SIZE:**
9,596,960 sq km

◉ **POPULATION:**
1,373,541,000

○ **CURRENCY:**
Chinese renminbi

● **CAPITAL:**
Beijing

○ **LANGUAGE:**
Chinese

Silken Secrets

China's signature fabric is silk. The secret of its manufacture from a protein in silkworm cocoons was discovered in around 2700 B.C.E. The penalty for revealing the secret to the outside world was death!

Territorial Disputes

Several regions within the PRC, including Tibet and Uighur, are autonomous – they govern themselves. Hong Kong and Macau are cities with special administrative status. This means these places govern themselves to some extent, but are not independent from China.

South Korea

ASIA

- ✷ South Koreans make more than 100 types of *kimchi* – a dish of fermented vegetables
- ✷ Automobiles and mobile phones are among South Korea's main exports

Occupying the southern end of the Korean Peninsula, I have three coasts. Between them, green rolling hills and mountains dominate my land. In the olden days, my cross-country communications were sent by *bongsu* – torchlight and smoke signals. The beacon mound on my Namsan Mountain is just one of many strategic signalling spots. Today, I prefer to communicate via the Internet, and the message is crystal clear: I am the "It" country of the 21st century.

K-Culture is exploding: K-pop fangirls dance their way in sync across the Asian continent and Seoul's Coex Centre is home to Asia's biggest underground shopping mall. Fortress remnants at Seoul and Hwaseong may testify to my ancient history, but I'm high-tech at heart. Almost half my population lives in and around my capital, and even those inhabiting my traditional wooden *hanok* (houses) have Wi-Fi. It's hardly surprising, since my Internet is the fastest in the world.

- ○ **SIZE:**
  99,720 sq km
- ● **POPULATION:**
  50,924,000
- ● **CURRENCY:**
  South Korean won
- ● **CAPITAL:**
  Seoul
- ○ **LANGUAGE:**
  Korean

North Korea

ASIA

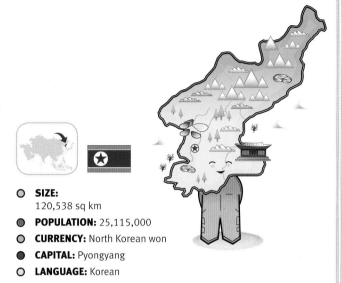

With two coasts, one on each side of the Korean Peninsula, I have access to plenty of seafood – molluscs and seaweed are specialties. And I am loaded with iron and coal deposits. My 670 c.e. P'yohun-sa Buddhist temple on Mount Kumgang is one of nearly 200 national treasures. But I have a dark side: my extreme government has keen interest in developing nuclear weapons, while many of my people live in extreme poverty.

- ○ **SIZE:** 120,538 sq km
- ● **POPULATION:** 25,115,000
- ○ **CURRENCY:** North Korean won
- ● **CAPITAL:** Pyongyang
- ○ **LANGUAGE:** Korean

Mongolia

ASIA

My land is mostly grassland plateau rimmed by mountains and desert. Colliding winds in my Badain Jaran desert create dual-horned barchan sand dunes! To keep the desert at bay, my yurt-dwelling nomadic herders plant native salt cedars and Siberian elm trees. I'm the fabled home of cashmere goats and the Mohawk-maned takhi, the world's only truly wild horse. My native music is played on a horse-head fiddle and features throat singing.

- ○ **SIZE:** 1,564,116 sq km
- ● **POPULATION:** 3,031,000
- ○ **CURRENCY:** Mongolian tögrög
- ● **CAPITAL:** Ulaanbaatar
- ○ **LANGUAGE:** Mongolian

Japan

ASIA

- ☀ At 3776 metres, the dormant volcano of Mount Fuji is Japan's highest mountain
- ☀ Kyoto's Kinkaku-ji temple (the Golden Pavilion) is coated in gold leaf
- ☀ The Shinkansen bullet train reaches speeds of 320 kilometres per hour

An archipelago, I comprise four main islands and nearly 6800 islets. Separated from the Asian mainland by more than 190 kilometres, I'm a tight-knit family unit: until recently, more than 98 per cent of my people were of "pure" Japanese heritage.

Although my terrain is a challenge to farm, I've mastered the art: for centuries, my mountain slopes have been shaped into graceful terraces that produce abundant rice in little space. Contemporary life relies less on agriculture, though: the urban sprawl of Tokyo, my capital since 1868, is home to around 31 million people.

Tokyo's Shibuya Crossing is said to be the world's most perfectly choreographed intersection, packed with pedestrians moving in sync, like a flock of swallows.

Pickled octopus, anyone? The sea and its bounty are a way of life here: I have one of the world's largest fishing fleets and my people consume more than one-tenth of the world's seafood. The Ama of Shima Peninsula are female free-divers who plunge under the waves to forage for shellfish. My traditional diet of rice, fish and pickled vegetables means my people live longer: I have a high percentage of centenarians.

- ○ **SIZE:**
  377,915 sq km
- ◑ **POPULATION:**
  126,702,000
- ○ **CURRENCY:**
  Japanese yen
- ● **CAPITAL:**
  Tokyo
- ○ **LANGUAGE:**
  Japanese

Ancient Ceremonies

When Japanese people get interested in a subject, they take it to the max! Writing poetry, drinking tea and even burning incense all have elaborate rituals and implements surrounding their practice.

Shinto

Japan's Shinto religion has no founder and no sacred texts. Instead, it honors *kami*, little spirits or gods of place, and the landscape is scattered with thousands of shrines to them. Foxes are seen as the magic messengers of Inari, the *kami* (god) of rice, tea and fertility. Fox statues often guard Inari shrines.

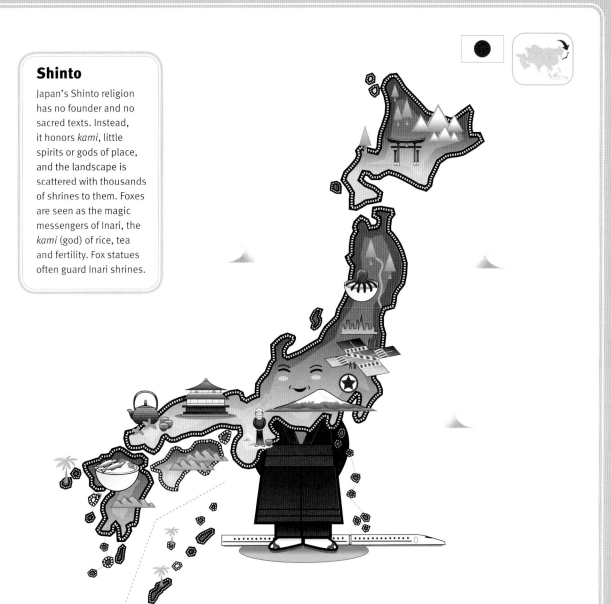

Myanmar

ASIA

A country with a colourful past, my former royal capital occupies a moated fortress in Mandalay; Yangon is full of golden pagodas and old colonial buildings; and Buddhists in saffron-yellow robes can be seen everywhere, especially at popular pagoda festivals. Tigers roam rainforests dense with hardwoods and fruit trees. My southern delta wetlands are home to turtle and crocodile sanctuaries, and great flocks of migrating birds.

- **SIZE:** 676,578 sq km
- **POPULATION:** 56,890,000
- **CURRENCY:** Myanmar kyat
- **CAPITAL:** Rangoon
- **LANGUAGE:** Burmese

Laos

ASIA

L uring travellers a-plenty, mine is a dramatic landscape of limestone cliffs and rivers. Abundant rain keeps my rice fields and tea plantations looking lush. I have no coast, but Vientiane, my "city of sandalwood", is on the Mekong River; people gather here to watch spectacular sunsets and enjoy the night market with bowls of *klao niaw* (sticky rice). Pha That Luang, the city's golden Buddhist stupa, has become a national emblem.

- **SIZE:** 236,800 sq km
- **POPULATION:** 7,019,000
- **CURRENCY:** Laotian kip
- **CAPITAL:** Vientiane
- **LANGUAGE:** Lao

Cambodia
ASIA

✺ Biannual monsoons bring more than three-quarters of the country's annual rainfall

✺ Cambodians eat plenty of fish – fresh, dried, smoked and salted

○ **SIZE:**
181,035 sq km

● **POPULATION:**
15,957,000

○ **CURRENCY:**
Cambodian riel

● **CAPITAL:**
Phnom Penh

○ **LANGUAGE:**
Khmer

Sure, the massive twining roots of kapok and strangler fig trees sprouting from my temple ruins at Ta Prohm are impressive. But my real religious gem is Angkor Wat, the monumental temple complex founded by Suryavarman II in the 12th century in honour of the Hindu god Vishnu. Three thousand *apsaras* (sacred nymphs) adorn its gateways. Their stories feature in the choreography of my Cambodian classical dancers.

The Mekong River flows south through my eastern region and much of my land is forested. My rosewood and resin trees are at risk, though: their wood is valuable, and my deforestation rate is one of the world's highest. My south-western Cardamom Mountains, named for their wild-growing spice, are home to elephants, gaur (wild cattle), Siamese crocodiles and pileated gibbons. Take care to avoid the cobras!

Thailand

ASIA

- More than 40,000 Buddhist temples dot the Thai landscape
- The native blind cavefish can shimmy its way straight up waterfalls

With gibbons cartwheeling through my teak treetops, a tradition of wandering forest monks and a beach party in full swing on my southern island of Phuket, I'd say the only resident getting a rest here is my massive reclining gold Buddha. Tradition says my Emerald Buddha (actually sculpted from jade) was revealed when lightning struck a Chiang Mai temple in the 15th century.

My diverse species are losing ground due to habitat loss, but what marvels they are! When my golden-necklaced sunbear unfurls his 25-centimetre-long tongue, it's mop-up time for termites and my clouded leopards are known for their now-you-see-them-now-you-don't presence in my deepest rainforest, said to be the world's oldest. My people are pistol-packing – water pistols, that is. During Songkran, my New Year festival, people wash away the past year's sins in a three-day-long water fight. To float away bad luck and honour the river goddess, they send candle-laden banana-leaf boats sailing down rivers.

SIZE:
513,120 sq km

POPULATION:
68,201,000

CURRENCY:
Thai baht

CAPITAL:
Bangkok

LANGUAGE:
Thai

Vietnam
ASIA

☀ Hang Son Doong Cave, the largest in the world, has its own river, jungle and climate
☀ Vietnam is the world's largest exporter of black pepper and cashew nuts

I'm a dreamy waterworld, shimmery and reflective. The beaches of my 3260-kilometre coastline are a tourist draw, but it's on the rivers, canals and flooded fields of my Mekong River delta that daily life flows. No parking lots here: even the markets are afloat, with narrow, lantern-hung boats piled high with local fish and fruits. Agricultural produce can be seen gracing household altars, where it joins other ritual items – joss sticks (incense), candles and photos of deceased ancestors.

Even my puppet shows are waterborne: "making puppets dance on water" is a tradition dating back to the 11th century. Water buffaloes, my iconic animal, used to plough fields and pull carts, are often tended by children. In Hanoi, Hoan Kiem Lake is the murky realm of Cua Rua (Grandfather), my sacred giant turtle. Near Fansipan, my highest mountain, Sapa rice terraces hand carved a thousand years ago are still tended by the Hmong, one of my hill tribes.

○ **SIZE:**
331,210 sq km

● **POPULATION:**
95,261,000

○ **CURRENCY:**
Vietnamese dong

● **CAPITAL:**
Hanoi

○ **LANGUAGE:**
Vietnamese

Malaysia

ASIA

- ☀ Malaysia's two regions are separated by 1030 kilometres of South China Sea
- ☀ *Nasi lemak* – coconut-milk-infused rice – is often served wrapped in a banana leaf

○ **SIZE:**
329,847 sq km

◉ **POPULATION:**
30,950,000

○ **CURRENCY:**
Malaysian ringgit

● **CAPITAL:**
Kuala Lumpur

○ **LANGUAGE:**
Bahasa Malaysia

Occupying both the Malay peninsula and the northern half of the island of Borneo, I like to spread myself out. I police the Malacca Strait, vital to shipping lanes linking the Indian and Pacific Oceans. Once a tiny tin-mining town, now my city Kuala Lumpur is a futuristic fantasia: the pedestrian bridge spanning the space between its twin Petronas Towers is 170 metres off the ground!

Edible nests cemented with bird spit are harvested from my vaulted Gomantong Caves. Prized for Chinese bird's nest soup, they fetch up to £1500 per kilo. I'm also home to the durian, the fruit with a shell like a spiny grenade and a smelly custard centre, and to betel nuts, a traditional gift to Malay brides on their wedding day. My main man of the forests, the orangutan, is humans' closest primate relative.

Philippines
ASIA

* Only one-third of the Philippines' 7000-plus islands are inhabited
* The endangered, 1-metre-tall Philippine eagle is the country's national bird

Between them, my mostly mountainous islands boast miles and miles of sandy coastline. But watch out – located on the Pacific's volcano-prone Ring of Fire, I'm a bit of a drama queen. In 1991, I gave in to a major meltdown, kicking up my cranky heels with the 20th-century's second-largest eruption (of Mount Pinatubo) and a typhoon (Yunya) at the very same time! The eruption sent an ash cloud 35 kilometres into the air, which combined with the typhoon's heavy rains to create lahars, very destructive flows of mud and ash. Waahh!

Much calmer now, I like to coo at my super-cute fauna. My adorable mouse deer, the chevrotain, tops the scales at just 7.5 kilograms. Can you smell buttered popcorn? That's just the natural aroma of my binturong, a slightly scruffy looking creature resembling a cross between a bear and a cat. My abacá trees produce a fibre known as Manila hemp; salt resistant, it's excellent for marine rope and fishing nets.

○ **SIZE:**
300,000 sq km

● **POPULATION:**
102,624,000

○ **CURRENCY:**
Philippine peso

● **CAPITAL:**
Manila

○ **LANGUAGES:**
Filipino, English

Indonesia

ASIA

* Indonesia has more than 100 active volcanoes; the best known is Krakatoa
* Deer Cave on Borneo has a bat population of some three million
* Lake Toba, in Sumatra, is the largest volcanic crater lake in the world

Island hop 'til you drop? You'll crash for sure if you try to visit all my islands: I've got around 17,000 of them, but only 8000 are inhabited. A beach bum centre of the universe? Don't be fooled . . . there's much more at stake! I have the world's largest Muslim population and fourth-largest population overall. My people speak a staggering 300 languages between them.

High populations almost always equal deforestation: people burn down the jungle to create palm-oil plantations or simply to plant subsistence crops. What's a Javan slow loris to do? These primates live in the forest canopy. On my big island of Sumatra, the Sumatran tiger is hanging on by a claw: aper companies want its habitat. Grrrr!

At least my native giant parasitic corpse flowers are doing well; their rotting-meat smell attracts flies, and that helps them get pollinated. Along with sweet-smelling jasmine and delicate moth orchids, they're my national flowers, but try putting all three in a bouquet . . . hmmm. Drumming is always good therapy, and that's where my gamelan orchestras of Java and Bali come in. The instruments, like the metallophone, are all played with mallets. Hammer away!

○ **SIZE:**
1,904,569 sq km

◉ **POPULATION:**
258,316,000

○ **CURRENCY:**
Indonesian rupiah

◉ **CAPITAL:**
Jakarta

○ **LANGUAGE:**
Bahasa Indonesia

Island Life

Indonesia's main islands fall into several groups: The Greater Sunda Islands of Sumatra, Java, southern Borneo, and Celebes; the Lesser Sunda Islands, which include Bali; the Moluccas; and New Guinea.

Temple Territory

Thousands of temples dot the Indonesian landscape. In Java, the 10th-century Prambanan complex includes three ornately decorated temples dedicated to the three great Hindu divinities (Shiva, Vishnu and Brahma). Pura Besakih, on the slopes of Mount Agung in Bali, features 23 temples.

Singapore

ASIA

- ☀ This cluster of small islands has two monsoon seasons: Nov–Mar and May–Sept
- ☀ Indigenous animals include slow lorises, long-tailed macaques and scaly anteaters

○ **SIZE:**
697 sq km

◐ **POPULATION:**
5,782,000

○ **CURRENCY:**
Singapore dollar

● **CAPITAL:**
Singapore

○ **LANGUAGES:**
Mandarin, English,
Malay, Tamil

A city-state at the southern tip of the Malay Peninsula, my low-elevation location has left me vulnerable to sea-level rise. It has also brought me great fortune. You see, my massive Port of Singapore sits at the mouth of the Malacca Strait, a stretch of water that has more than 40 per cent of the world's sea traffic passing through it. I'm expert at the computer logistics needed to wrangle all that traffic, at maritime law and ship brokerage. I've invested in some pretty eye-catching architecture – check out my lotus-blossom-shaped ArtScience Museum and my vertical gardens, which feature a grove of 18 solar-powered, energy-producing "super trees" that weave ferns and tropical plants into their branched steel structure. My famous half-lion/half-fish Merlion fountain at the mouth of the Singapore River symbolizes my status as a lion of the sea.

Brunei

ASIA

Adiddy sovereign state on the north coast of Borneo, my land consists of two unconnected halves. Oil and gas have made me rich; the sultan's home, Istana Nurul Iman, is the largest residential palace in the world. You try finding your way around 1788 rooms, 257 bathrooms and a stable for 200 polo ponies! In my lowland tropical rainforest, my proboscis monkey is easy to spot, with its 10-centimetre-long hooter.

- ○ **SIZE:** 5765 sq km
- ◉ **POPULATION:** 437,000
- ◉ **CAPITAL:** Bandar Seri Begawan
- ○ **CURRENCY:** Bruneian dollar
- ○ **LANGUAGE:** Malay

East Timor

ASIA

Gaining independence from Indonesia in 2002, I'm the 21st-century's first sovereign state. Rugged and mountainous, I form half of the island of Timor, home to hot springs and villages with thatch-roofed houses. Coffee, cinnamon and cocoa love my tropical climate. Around me lie beautiful coral reefs with barracuda, dugongs and reef sharks swimming in the clear waters. My national park protects wildlife, such as the endangered yellow-crested cockatoo.

- ○ **SIZE:** 14,874 sq km
- ◉ **POPULATION:** 1,261,000
- ◉ **CAPITAL:** Dili
- ○ **CURRENCY:** U.S. dollar
- ○ **LANGUAGES:** Tetum, Portuguese

Oceania

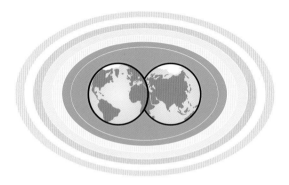

I've got more ground than you think – it's just that a lot of it is having a good long soak beneath the Pacific Ocean. A bathymetric map – that's a map showing underwater terrain – would tell the tale: New Zealand may look like two skinny islands bathing in the South Pacific, but that's just the bits that decided to get some fresh air. Idling beneath the waves is a land mass the size of India, known as Zealandia. My other major landmasses are Australia and New Guinea. What goes on underwater, though, doesn't always stay there: it's all about tectonic temper tantrums. When the deep layers of the Earth get hot under the crusty collar, plates start crashing, super-continents split up and volcanic islands spit up from the ocean floor: my Melanesian islands are all volcanic.

- ☀ **Land mass:** 8,525,989 sq km
- ☀ **Number of countries:** 14
- ☀ **Biggest lake:** Eyre
- ☀ **Longest river:** Murray
- ☀ **Highest mountain:** Puncak Jaya

Oceania

Australia

Fiji

Kiribati

Marshall Islands

Micronesia

Nauru

New Zealand

Palau

Papua New Guinea

Samoa

Solomon Islands

Tonga

Tuvalu

Vanuatu

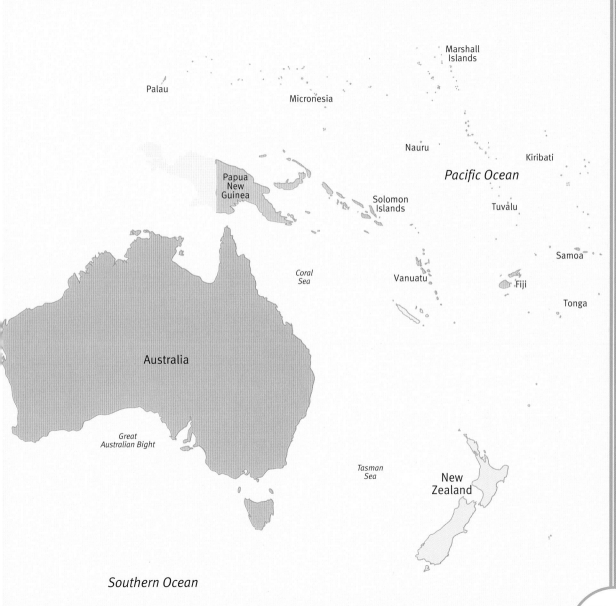

Marshall
Islands

Palau

Micronesia

Nauru

Pacific Ocean

Kiribati

*Papua
New
Guinea*

Solomon
Islands

Tuvalu

Coral
Sea

Vanuatu

Samoa

Fiji

Tonga

Australia

Great
Australian Bight

Tasman
Sea

New
Zealand

Southern Ocean

Australia

OCEANIA

* Sydney Opera House's roofline is shaped like a series of shimmering "sails"
* New South Wales lays claim to some of the world's best surfing beaches
* Tasmania's fragrant Huon pine trees can grow to be 2500 years old

My outback will always be upfront in my popular image, but there's more to me than rusty red dirt, salt scrub bushes and kangaroos. Secluded in the South Pacific, I'm roamed by a good number of strange species that reflect my biodiversity. Echidnas and platypuses, for example, are the world's only monotremes (that's egg-laying mammals to you). My Great Dividing Range hugs the contours of my east coast and the ancient Flinders Ranges rise up in my south. In Western Australia and my Northern Territory, you'll find the world's two largest monoliths (massive rocks), Mount Augustus and Uluru (Ayer's Rock). For my native Aborigines, whose Dreaming stories revolve around the natural world, Uluru has long been held a sacred site.

Would you believe that almost 70 per cent of my territory is desert and mostly low-lying? I'm also of two minds about trees: in my south-west, there's the Nullarbor Plain – the name means "no trees" in Latin – but in my Queensland province, I boast the Daintree – the Earth's oldest tropical rainforest. The Nullarbor is the site of the 5500-kilometre-long Great Barrier Fence: the world's longest, built to keep predatory dingoes away from sheep!

SIZE:
7,741,220 sq km

POPULATION:
22,993,000

CURRENCY:
Australian dollar

CAPITAL:
Canberra

LANGUAGE:
English

Bush Tucker

Bush tucker is Aussie speak for the country's nourishing native plants, berries and fruits. They include riberries, muntries (great in chutneys), sandalwood nuts, cinnamon myrtle and blood limes.

The Great Barrier Reef

The world's largest coral reef lies offshore of Queensland. Vast and colourful, it is home to 600 types of corals, 100 species of jellyfish and 3000 different molluscs, sharks, rays, dolphins and dugongs. Recent rises in sea temperatures have caused areas of the reef to die off.

New Zealand

OCEANIA

- ☀ Some 27 million sheep live in New Zealand; six for each member of the population
- ☀ Commercial bungee jumping is said to have originated in New Zealand
- ☀ Great Barrier Island is home to hot springs, where you can bathe

Very far away from anywhere else, I lie 1500 kilometres south-east of Australia, separated by the Tasman Sea. Consider me top tramping territory! My North Island features mountains running down the centre, with rich farmland on either side. Sheep love to graze here and are the source of my cosy New Zealand wool. My South Island's massive Southern Alps give way to Fiordland, which combines mountain, glacier, fjord and rainforest biomes! The Alps run onto a wide stretch called the Canterbury Plains, farmland formed by alluvial deposit – runoff from the mountains. Offshore, Stewart Island is home to penguins and my national bird, the kiwi.

My species evolved in total isolation out here, and so many of them are seriously strange – like *Powelliphanta*, an egg-laying, carnivorous snail that sucks up earthworms like spaghetti and can live up to 20 years. My native tuatara reptile has a third eye on top of its head that's like a clock – it helps know the time of day and the tuatara season!

I have urban attractions, too, such as Auckland's Sky Tower, which reaches 328 metres skyward – my tallest building. And, of course, there is the Beehive in Wellington. Part of my parliamentary complex, it looks . . . well, like a beehive!

- ○ **SIZE:**
  268,838 sq km
- ◓ **POPULATION:**
  4,475,000
- ○ **CURRENCY:**
  New Zealand dollar
- ● **CAPITAL:**
  Wellington
- ○ **LANGUAGES:**
  English, Maori

Flightless Birds

New Zealand has the most species of flightless birds, including the kiwi and the penguin. Before humans, birds had no predators on land, and without any need to make an escape, they lost their ability to fly.

The Maoris

My native people call me Aotearoa, "Land of the Long White Cloud," for my misty mountain ranges. Polynesian people who first beached their canoes on my shores around 1000 C.E., Maoris are known for their *tamoko* (swirly tattoos) chiselled into the skin, and for the *haka*, a grunting and grimacing war dance.

Papua New Guinea

OCEANIA

- ✳ Each of the 700 Papuan and Melanesian tribes speaks its own language
- ✳ Asaro "mudmen" re-create warrior ancestors wearing huge mud masks

○ **SIZE:**
462,840 sq km

◉ **POPULATION:**
6,791,000

○ **CURRENCY:**
Papua New Guinean kina

● **CAPITAL:**
Port Moresby

○ **LANGUAGES:**
Tok Pisin, English,
Hiri Motu

Is that a crocodile tickling my toes? My 80,000-square-kilometre, largely unexplored Sepik River basin is known for tribes who hunt crocodiles. They submerge themselves in river vegetation and rummage in the mud with their bare hands and feet!

A resource-rich land covered by rain and cloud forests, I have a central mountain range – the Highlands – and at least 100 volcanoes.

But lava is not the only danger here. Growing 1.8 metres tall, my blue-necked cassowary, a bird, can deliver a nasty blow with its lethal, dagger-like claw. Better to stick with my spotted cuscus, a cat-sized, ginger-dappled possum. My Anga tribespeople mummify respected elders in a complex smoking ritual and place them on cliffs overlooking their villages as a comforting link to the world of ancestor spirits.

Marshall Islands

OCEANIA

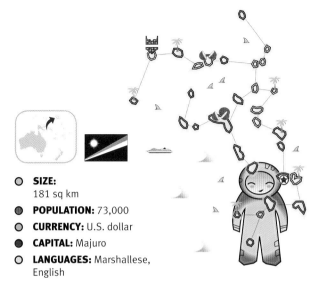

My territory includes many scattered islands, but also atolls. These rings of land around lagoons are the scant remains of extinct volcanoes. You might have heard of my atoll Bikini, which means land of the coconuts. Its name was adopted by a French fashion designer for a teeny two-piece swimming suit. But be careful if you swim in my waters; I have the world's largest shark sanctuary – four times the size of California.

- ○ **SIZE:** 181 sq km
- ● **POPULATION:** 73,000
- ○ **CURRENCY:** U.S. dollar
- ● **CAPITAL:** Majuro
- ○ **LANGUAGES:** Marshallese, English

Palau

OCEANIA

Saltwater crocodiles lounge in the mangrove swamps of my hot and rainy islands. You might also see crab-eating macaques. Locals picnic by the monolithic stones at Badrulchau, on my Babeldaob Island and divers plunge into pristine waters around my coral reefs and wartime shipwrecks. At Koror, you can swim with trained dolphins at Dolphin Pacific, the largest dolphin research centre in the world.

- ○ **SIZE:** 459 sq km
- ● **POPULATION:** 21,000
- ○ **CURRENCY:** U.S. dollar
- ● **CAPITAL:** Ngerulmud
- ○ **LANGUAGES:** Palauan, English

Kiribati

OCEANIA

Straddling the Equator and the international date line, my Millennium Island is the first place in the world to celebrate New Year. Getting to many of my white-sand beaches involves sailing there. Try a Kiribati canoe, built traditionally without using screws or nails. The Phoenix Island Protected Area is the largest marine conservation site in the world; see if you can spot the endangered Phoenix petrel, just one of my many seabirds.

○ **SIZE:** 811 sq km
◉ **POPULATION:** 107,000
○ **CURRENCY:** Kiribati dollar
● **CAPITAL:** Tarawa
○ **LANGUAGES:** Gilbertese, English

Micronesia

OCEANIA

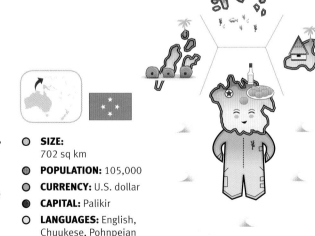

My many islands make up four states whose traditional meeting houses have high pointed roofs. On the island of Yap, huge stones called Rai have holes carved in the middle and once acted as currency. You might enjoy green tangerines, whereas *sakau*, a drink made from the root of the kava plant, is an acquired taste. My largest city is on Chuuk Lagoon where more than 250 fish varieties swim among 80 coral-encrusted World War II shipwrecks.

○ **SIZE:** 702 sq km
◉ **POPULATION:** 105,000
○ **CURRENCY:** U.S. dollar
● **CAPITAL:** Palikir
○ **LANGUAGES:** English, Chuukese, Pohnpeian

Samoa

OCEANIA

- Extensive body tattoos are considered a mark of man- or womanhood
- Staple foods include *copra* (dried coconut), cocoa beans and bananas

○ **SIZE:**
2831 sq km

● **POPULATION:**
199,000

○ **CURRENCY:**
Samoan tala

● **CAPITAL:**
Apia

○ **LANGUAGE:**
Samoan

Welcome to my small archipelago dominated by two large central South Pacific islands. I am the product of ancient volcanic activity; today only my westernmost Savai'i island boasts live volcanoes: Mata o le Afi, Mount Matavanu and Mauga Afi.

Hungry for a coral palolo worm or two? This seasonal delicacy rises to the sea surface just once a year to spawn, only to be netted and noshed on the spot by locals! My Teuila Festival, named for my red ginger flowers, celebrates Fa'a Samoa, or the Samoan way. Events include *fa'ataupati*, an all-male dance that imitates the gyrations used to smack my voracious mosquitoes. Mosquitoes aside, Europeans find me an island paradise: Robert Louis Stevenson, author of *Treasure Island* and *Kidnapped*, spent his happiest years on my large island, Upolu.

Tonga

OCEANIA

My archipelago stretches some 800 kilometres, but most people live on Tongatapu, home to the royal palace. You might see a flying fox here – actually it is a bat and considered sacred, or *tabu* (the origin of the word "taboo"). Tongans like to eat, and their feasts may consist of dozens of dishes, particularly suckling pig and steamed fish. Obesity has traditionally been seen as attractive, but men must keep their shirts on in public.

- **SIZE:** 747 sq km
- **POPULATION:** 107,000
- **CURRENCY:** Tongan Pa'anga
- **CAPITAL:** Nuku'alofa
- **LANGUAGES:** Tongan, English

Fiji

OCEANIA

Tourists visit me for my romantic white beaches; honeymooners head for my island resorts with thatched-roofed huts called *bure*. Covered in forests, my tropical islands are producers of sugar cane, coconuts and copra. Elsewhere, you'll find cane toads, iguanas, geckos and turtles among my reptiles. Fijians are hooked on rugby, and the national team is known for performing a *Cibi*, a traditional war dance, before a match.

- **SIZE:** 18,274 sq km
- **POPULATION:** 915,000
- **CURRENCY:** Fijian dollar
- **CAPITAL:** Suva
- **LANGUAGES:** English, Fijian, Hindi

Solomon Islands

OCEANIA

* Lake Tegano, on Rennell Island, is the largest of all Pacific Island lakes
* A WWII shipwreck breaks through the surface of the sea north of Honiara

○ **SIZE:**
28,896 sq km

◉ **POPULATION:**
635,000

○ **CURRENCY:**
Solomon Islands dollar

◉ **CAPITAL:**
Honiara

○ **LANGUAGES:**
English, Melanesian Pidgin

Defending biodiversity is my passion – it would have to be, given my six large and nearly 1000 small islands. My Arnavon island group is a major nesting site for hawksbill sea turtles: every year, my sand skitters as hundreds of little hatchlings scramble their way out of nests and head for the sea. My cosy, warm volcanic sand serves as a babysitter for the megapode, or incubator bird, who lays its eggs in thermal sand burrows, so the mother doesn't have to sit on a nest. My money was once made of bird feathers: fibre coils wrapped in red feathers from the scarlet honeyeater.

The children from my islands are expert canoers: who needs a bicycle when you've got an outrigger canoe and plenty of lagoons to paddle through? At sundown, music sounds from pan pipes, or bamboo flutes and slit drums.

Nauru

OCEANIA

I'm tiny – you can walk around me in a few hours, admiring the coral pinnacles off my coast. And I'm exhausted, too. You see, phosphates – seabird droppings that once made me the second-richest country in the world – are all but mined out now. Seabirds still come here, though, to rest on their long flights: noddies are caught and eaten, and frigate birds are trapped and tamed. I'm not far from Australia, and Australian-rules football is my most popular sport.

○ **SIZE:**
21 sq km
◉ **POPULATION:** 10,000
○ **CURRENCY:** Australian dollar
● **CAPITAL:** Yaren
○ **LANGUAGES:** Nauruan, English

Vanuatu

OCEANIA

Forgive me if my tummy rumbles . . . earthquakes and volcanoes, such as the dramatic Yasur on my island of Tanna, often shake my archipelago. No wonder many reality-TV survivor programs have been set here! I am hot and rainy nine months of the year, so scuba divers find my waters warm and welcoming. Horseback riding is popular, too. Cattle are my most important livestock, though pigs are considered a sign of wealth – more so if they have tusks.

○ **SIZE:**
12,189 sq km
◉ **POPULATION:** 278,000
○ **CURRENCY:** Vanuatu vatu
● **CAPITAL:** Port Vila
○ **LANGUAGES:** Bislama, French, English

Tuvalu

OCEANIA

* Te Ano is a national game – a little like volleyball; it has two balls in play at a time
* Tuvaluan women make jewellery from cowrie (sea-snail) shells

Remote? I've heard that word before. It's true, you'll squint to see me on a map of the South Pacific, riding the waves about 4000 kilometres north-east of Australia. My name means "eight standing together", for my eight low-lying atolls, none more than 4.5 metres above sea level. Flooding is a real problem. My people know their land could be submerged, and they've taken the initiative to reduce dependence on imported diesel and increase use of wind and solar for power instead.

Weird, but fresh water can be a problem here, too, because there are no rivers – so rainfall is crucial. My only native mammal is a rat. Sure, you'll see chickens, goats, pigs and dogs, but they are all imported. My people are mostly subsistence farmers, growing coconut palms, breadfruit trees and bananas. The rate of fish consumption here is one of the world's highest – duh! Tuvaluans fish from hand-crafted canoes, using butterfly nets to catch flying fish.

○ **SIZE:**
26 sq km

◉ **POPULATION:**
11,000

○ **CURRENCY:** Tuvaluan or Australian dollar

◉ **CAPITAL:**
Funafuti

○ **LANGUAGES:**
Tuvaluan, English

Glossary

Annex – to take control of a region or country and make it part of another region or country.

Archipelago – a group of neighbouring islands and/or islets within the same body of water.

Arid – dry, barren.

Atoll – a ring-shaped coral reef, island or group of islets surrounding a lagoon.

Autonomous – independent, self-governing.

Biodiversity – the variety of life-forms within a particular habitat, ecosystem or country.

Biome – a community of plants and animals living in a particular physical environment.

Camel caravan – traders or tribes-people riding a line of camels packed with trade goods or possessions across a desert landscape.

Cassava – a tropical plant cultivated for its root; cassava flour (for bread), tapioca pudding and even laundry starch are made from the root.

Cataract – a large waterfall that falls over a precipice as opposed to falling over rocks.

Civil war – a war between groups of people who are citizens of the same country.

Colony – a country or region under the political control of another, usually distant, country.

Communism – a political system in which major resources such as mines, factories and farms are owned by the state, and wealth is divided equally among citizens.

Delta – an area of wetlands that forms at the mouth of a river, where it empties into a larger body of water.

El Niño – an irregularly occurring flow of unusually warm surface water off the western coast of South America that disrupts normal weather patterns.

Elevation – the distance of an area of land above sea level.

Emirate – an area ruled by an emir – a type of leader – in some Islamic countries.

Epicentre – the very central point of something; especially, the location where the greatest damage from an earthquake occurs.

Erosion – the wearing away of material, such as earth or rock, by the constant flow of water or wind.

EU – European Union; association of European nations formed in 1993 to promote political and economic integration.

Export – to sell, or transport for sale, goods and services outside the country in which the goods or services are produced.

Fauna – the native animals of a given region.

Federation – a central political authority formed by smaller groups (such as countries, states, or counties) that give up some individual power to the federation.

Fertile – describes rich soil or land that is able to produce abundant crops.

Fjord – a long, narrow inlet of the sea surrounded by steep cliffs, common in Norway and Iceland; usually cut by glaciers.

Fortification – a defensive wall, moat, bank or fort; a construction built for defence.

Fumarole – a vent in the Earth's surface that releases hot vapour, steam and/or gases.

Geothermal power – heat from the Earth's interior converted into an energy source, such as steam used to power a turbine generator.

Glacier – a large ice mass that moves very slowly over land.

Hominid – a primate mammal that stands erect on two feet; hominids include humans, human ancestors and some great apes.

Hydroelectric power – electrical power produced through the use of the gravitational force of flowing water.

Indigenous – originating in, or native to, a particular place.

Irrigation – supplying water by artificial means: for example, watering a field by underground water piping.

Karst – an area of land formed from dissolvable rock, such as limestone, usually featuring underground drainage systems with sink holes and caves.

Lagoon – a shallow body of saltwater separated from the ocean by sand bars, barrier islands or coral reefs.

Landlocked – a country almost, or entirely, surrounded by land; having no coastline.

Latrine – a very basic toilet.

Magma – molten rock usually located deep beneath the Earth's crust that occasionally comes to the surface through cracks in the crust or through the eruption of volcanoes.

Mangroves – salt-tolerant tropical trees with densely tangled, above-ground root systems; they help to stabilize coastlines by protecting them from flooding.

Marsupial – a mammal that bears immature babies, then carries them in a belly pouch.

Mesa – an isolated flat-topped hill with steep sides.

Mineral – a material that is neither animal nor plant, and which makes up the Earth's rocks soils, and sands.

Migratory – describes animals or people who move from one place to another for work, grazing, weather, or to reach better economic or survival conditions.

Mineral ore – a natural deposit of a mineral in rock, from which metal can be extracted, for example cassiterite (an ore of tin).

Mono-cropping – growing the same crop every year on the same land; the opposite of crop rotation; often reduces soil fertility.

Monsoon – usually in Southeast Asia, a reversal in the direction of the prevailing (strongest) winds that brings heavy rainfall.

NATO – a pact formed in 1949 by many North American and European nations, providing for mutual defence if a member nation is attacked.

Nomadic – having no fixed home; often native tribes who migrate according to seasons for better grazing or hunting and gathering.

Oasis – a small fertile area in the middle of a desert, with a water source, such as a spring.

Outpost – a settlement, town or camp that is established far away from the centre of things.

Paleolithic – of or relating to the time during the early Stone Age when people made rough tools and weapons out of stone; about 2 to 2.5 million years ago.

Pastoral – describes activities related to livestock raising and people whose occupation is herding livestock.

Peninsula – a piece of land almost entirely surrounded by water but connected to the mainland on one side.

Petroglyph – an image or symbol (usually prehistoric) carved into rock.

Plain – a large, flat area of land with few trees.

Plateau – an area of high, level ground.

Poacher – a person who kills wildlife illegally to sell to others.

Porous – easy to pass through; especially, a material full of pores (holes) that allow air or water to travel through.

Prairie – a large, open grassland region.

Primate – a member of a highly developed mammal group, including humans, monkeys, gorillas and chimpanzees.

Primeval – of, or relating to, earliest times.

Promontory – a high point of land or rock that projects into a body of water.

Rain shadow – an area of land that is desert because mountains block rainy weather.

Renewable – something (often an energy source) that is not depleted (used up, destroyed) when used.

Salt flat – a salt-encrusted area of land, often formed as a result of evaporation of a former body of water.

Savannah – grassy tropical or subtropical plain.

Shaman – a priest or priestess who acts as a go-between between the mortal and spirit worlds.

Sirocco – a hot dry wind blowing from North Africa and affecting southern Europe.

Soviet Union – Union of Soviet Socialist Republics, from 1922 to 1991, a one-party Communist state.

Super-continent – an ancient large continent or landmass thought to have consisted of modern continents before they broke apart.

Sustainable – a method of harvesting that prevents a resource becoming depleted or permanently damaged.

Tabletop mountain – a flat-topped, steep-sided mountain.

Taiga – a coniferous forest in high northern latitudes dominated by fir and spruce trees.

Tectonic plate – a sub-layer of the Earth's crust that moves, floats and sometimes fractures, and whose movement causes continental drift, earthquakes, volcanoes and mountains.

Terrain – the physical features of land, such as hills, valleys, rocky ledges, forested areas and streams.

Topography – the physical or natural features of a landscape.

Tundra – a vast, flat, treeless Arctic region of Europe, Asia and North America, in which the subsoil is permanently frozen.

Typhoon – both typhoon and hurricane are regional terms for tropical cyclones.

Voodoo – a religion that believes all natural things, living or not, have souls that can influence worldy events.

Weathering – the natural effects of time and the elements on an object, person or place.

Index

Numbers in **bold** indicate country entries